Julius Caesar

WILLIAM SHAKESPEARE

PRESTWICK HOUSE
LITERARY TOUCHSTONE CLASSICS™
P.O. BOX 658 • CLAYTON, DELAWARE 19938

Senior Editor: Paul Moliken

Editors: Elizabeth Osborne, Katherine Mayberry, Sarah Enloe, Jeremy Fiebig,
and Sarah Ann Ill

Design: Larry Knox

Production: Jerry Clark

Prestwick House
Literary Touchstone Classics

P.O. Box 658
Clayton, Delaware 19938
Tel: 1.800.932.4593
Fax: 1.888.718.9333
Web: www.prestwickhouse.com

AMERICAN^{SM}
SHAKESPEARE

CENTER
BLACKFRIARS PLAYHOUSE
STAUNTON • VIRGINIA

13 West Beverly Street
Staunton, Virginia 24401
Tel: 1.540.885.558
Fax: 1.540.885.4886

ISBN: 978-1-58049-587-5

CONTENTS

Strategies for Understanding Shakespeare's Language

1. **When reading verse, note the appropriate phrasing and intonation.**

   DO NOT PAUSE AT THE END OF A LINE unless there is a mark of punctuation. Shakespearean verse has a rhythm of its own, and once a reader gets used to it, the rhythm becomes very natural to speak in and read. Beginning readers often find it helpful to read a short pause at a comma and a long pause for a period, colon, semicolon, dash, or question mark.

   Here's an example from *The Merchant of Venice*, Act IV, Scene i:

   The quality of mercy is not strain'd, *(short pause)*
   It droppeth as the gentle rain from heaven
   Upon the place beneath: *(long pause)* it is twice blest; *(long pause)*
   It blesseth him that gives, *(short pause)* and him that takes; *(long pause)*
   'Tis mightiest in the mighties; *(long pause)* it becomes
   The throned monarch better than his crown; *(long pause)*

2. **Reading from punctuation mark to punctuation mark for meaning.**

   In addition to helping you read aloud, punctuation marks define units of thought. Try to understand each unit as you read, keeping in mind that periods, colons, semicolons, and question marks signal the end of a thought. Here's an example from *The Taming of the Shrew*:

   > Luc. Tranio, I saw her coral lips to move,
   >   And with her breath she did perfume the air;
   >   Sacred, and sweet, was all I saw in her.
   > Tra. Nay, then, 't is time to stir him from his
   >   trance.
   >   I pray, awake, sir: if you love the maid,
   >   Bend thoughts and wits to achieve her. (I,i)

   The first unit of thought is from "Tranio" to "air":
   He saw her lips move, and her breath perfumed the air.

   The second thought ("Sacred, and sweet...") re-emphasizes the first.

   Tranio replies that Lucentio needs to awaken from his trance and try to win "the maid." These two sentences can be considered one unit of thought.

3. In an **inverted sentence**, the verb comes before the subject. Some lines will be easier to understand if you put the subject first and reword the sentence. For example, look at the line below:

"Never was seen so black a day as this:" (*Romeo and Juliet, IV, v*)

You can change its inverted pattern so it is more easily understood:

"A day as black as this was never seen:"

4. An **ellipsis** occurs when a word or phrase is left out. In *Romeo and Juliet*, Benvolio asks Romeo's father and mother if they know the problem that is bothering their son. Romeo's father answers:

*"I neither know **it** nor can learn of **him**"* (*Romeo and Juliet I,i*).

This sentence can easily be understood to mean,

"I neither know [the cause of] it,
nor can [I] learn [about it from] him."

5. As you read longer speeches, keep track of the subject, verb, and object – *who* did *what* to *whom*.

In the clauses below, note the subject, verbs, and objects.

Ross: The king hath happily received, Macbeth,
    The news of thy success: and when he reads
    Thy personal venture in the rebel's fight… (*Macbeth* I, iii)

1ˢᵗ clause: *The king hath happily received, Macbeth,/The news of thy success:*
SUBJECT – The king
VERB – has received
OBJECT – the news [of Macbeth's success]
2ⁿᵈ clause: *and when he reads/thy personal venture in the rebel's fight,*

SUBJECT – he [the king]
        VERB – reads
        OBJECT – [about] your venture

In addition to following the subject, verb, and object of a clause, you also need to track pronoun references. In the following soliloquy Romeo, who is madly in love with Juliet, secretly observes her as she steps out on her balcony. To help you keep track of the pronoun references, we've made margin notes. (Note that the feminine pronoun sometimes refers to Juliet, but sometimes does not.)
But, soft! what light through yonder window breaks?
It is the east, and Juliet is the sun!
Arise, fair sun, and kill the envious moon,
Who* is already sick and pale with grief,   *"Who" refers to the moon.*

That thou her* maid art more fair than she:*   *"thou her maid" refers to Juliet,*
the sun.
"she" and "her" refer to the moon.

In tracking the line of action in a passage, it is useful to identify the main thoughts that are being expressed and paraphrase them. Note the following passage in which Hamlet expresses his feelings about the death of his father and the remarriage of his mother:

> O God! a beast that wants discourse of reason
> Would have mourn'd longer – married with my uncle,
> My father's brother, but no more like my father
> Than I to Hercules. (I,ii)

Paraphrasing the three main points, we find that Hamlet is saying:

- a mindless beast would have mourned the death of its mate longer than my mother did
- she married my uncle, my father's brother
- my uncle is not at all like my father

If you are having trouble understanding Shakespeare, the first rule is to read it out loud, just as an actor rehearsing would have to do. That will help you understand how one thought is connected to another.

6. Shakespeare frequently uses metaphor to illustrate an idea in a unique way. Pay careful attention to the two dissimilar objects or ideas being compared. In *Macbeth*, Duncan, the king says:
> I have begun to plant thee, and will labour
> To make thee full of growing. (I,v)

The king compares Macbeth to a tree he can plant and watch grow.

7. An *allusion* is a reference to some event, person, place, or artistic work, not directly explained or discussed by the writer; it relies on the reader's familiarity with the item referred to. Allusion is a quick way of conveying information or presenting an image. In the following lines, Romeo alludes to Diana, goddess of the hunt and of chastity, and to Cupid's arrow (love).

> ROMEO: Well, in that hit you miss: she'll not be hit
> with Cupid's arrow, she hath Dian's wit;
> and in strong proof of chastity well arm'd (I,i)

8. Contracted words are words in which a letter has been left out. Some that frequently appear:

be't	on't	wi'
do't	t'	'sblood
'gainst	ta'en	i'
'tis	e'en	
'bout	know'st	'twill
ne'er	o'	o'er

9. Archaic, obsolete and familiar words with unfamiliar definitions may also cause problems.

- **Archaic Words** Some archaic words, like *thee, thou, thy*, and *thine,* are instantly understandable, while others, like *betwixt,* cause a momentary pause.
- **Obsolete Words** If it were not for the notes in a Shakespeare text, obsolete words could be a problem; words like "beteem" are usually not found in student dictionaries. In these situations, however, a quick glance at the book's notes will solve the problem.
- **Familiar Words with Unfamiliar Definitions** Another problem is those familiar words whose definitions have changed. Because readers think they know the word, they do not check the notes. For example, in this comment from *Much Ado About Nothing*, the word *an* means *if*:
    > **Beatrice:** Scratching could not make it worse, *an* 'twere such a face as yours were. (I,i)

    For this kind of word, we have included margin notes.

10. Wordplay: puns, double entendres, and malapropisms

- A *pun* is a literary device that achieves humor or emphasis by playing on ambiguities. Two distinct meanings are suggested either by the same word or by two similar-sounding words.
- A *double entendre* is a kind of pun in which a word or phrase has a second, usually sexual, meaning.
- A *malapropism* occurs when a character mistakenly uses a word that he or she has confused with another word. In *Romeo and Juliet,* the Nurse tells Romeo that she needs to have a "confidence" with him, when she should have said "conference." Mockingly, Benvolio then says she probably will "indite" (rather than "invite") Romeo to dinner.

11. **Shakespeare's Language**

Our final word on Shakespeare's language is adapted by special permission from Ralph Alan Cohen's forthcoming book *Shakesfear and How to Cure It—A Guide to Teaching Shakespeare.*

What's so hard about Shakespeare's language? Many students come to Shakespeare's language assuming that the language of his period is substantially different from ours. In fact 98% of the words in Shakespeare are current-usage English words. So why does it sometimes seem hard to read Shakespeare? There are three main reasons:

- Originally, Shakespeare wrote the words for an actor to illustrate them as he spoke. In short, the play you have at hand was meant for the stage, not for the page.

- Shakespeare had the same love of reforming and rearranging words in such places as hip-hop and sportscasting today. His plays reflect an excitement about language and an inventiveness that becomes enjoyable once the reader gets into the spirit of it.

- Since Shakespeare puts all types of people on stage, those characters will include some who are pompous, some who are devious, some who are boring, and some who are crazy, and all of these will speak in ways that are sometimes trying. Modern playwrights creating similar characters have them speak in similarly challenging ways.

Stage Directions:

Prestwick House and the American Shakespeare Center share the belief that Shakespeare's stagecraft went hand-in-hand with his wordcraft. For that reason, we believe it is important for the reader to know which stage directions are modern and which derive from Shakespeare's earliest text—the single-play Quartos or the Folio, the first collected works (1623). All stage directions appear in italics, but the brackets enclose modern additions to the stage directions. Readers may assume that the unbracketed stage directions appear in the Quarto and/or Folio versions of the play.

Scene Locations:

Shakespeare imagined his play, first and foremost, on the stage of his outdoor or indoor theatre. The original printed versions of the plays do not give imaginary scene locations, except when they are occasionally mentioned in the dialogue. As an aid to the reader, this edition *does* include scene locations at the beginning of each scene, but puts all such locations in brackets to remind the reader that *this is not what Shakespeare envisioned and only possibly what he imagined.* Because the Folio has only act divisions, we have bracketed all scene divisions.

Reading Pointers for Sharper Insights

As you read, look for the themes and elements described below.

Personal vs. public responsibility: Throughout the play, Brutus comes across opportunities to seize power, but he always weighs them against his belief in the "general good." What does Caesar think about this general good? What kinds of things does he consider before making a decision?

Pragmatism vs. idealism: Cassius and Antony are shrewd politicians; they make plans after weighing the risks and benefits. Brutus, however, is an idealist, motivated only by his love of Rome and his strong convictions. In fact, Brutus meets his tragic end because of his idealism—a fact that even his enemies realize. He is too noble to survive in the corrupt and violent Rome that he has helped create.

Omens/Fate vs. Free Will: Plutarch, the Roman author who wrote *The Life of Julius Caesar* (upon which Shakespeare's play is based), often mentions *omens*—signs of things to come. On the day of Caesar's assassination, for instance, the *augurers* (priests who predict the future by examining the organs of birds and animals) supposedly found no heart in their sacrificed beast.
Shakespeare brings out his characters' views on destiny and free will by showing their belief, or lack of belief, in omens. Note any mention of the following:

- alignments of the stars
- meteors
- unusual animals
- ghosts

How do Caesar, Brutus, and Cassius interpret these signs?

Honor vs. Power: Cassius believes that political power must be taken by cunning and force; to him, it is an end in itself. Honor is Brutus' motivating force; he feels that power is, at best, a tool, and at worst, a burden.

Problems with democracy: The masses are fickle, and can be incited to riot. On the other hand, autocracy is dangerous. Even the most noble men can be corrupted by power.

Tragic flaw: a weakness in a character that leads to his or her destruction. Brutus' tragic flaw is his inability to confront reality.

Rhetoric: Notice how the art of verbal persuasion is both used and abused. Antony can completely reverse a situation by appealing to the plebians' emotions; Decius can change Caesar's mind by playing on his pride.

Julius Caesar

WILLIAM SHAKESPEARE

DRAMATIS PERSONAE

JULIUS CAESAR, Roman statesman and general
OCTAVIUS, Triumvir after Caesar's death, later Augustus Caesar, first emperor of Rome
MARCUS ANTONIUS, general and friend of Caesar, a Triumvir after his death
LEPIDUS, third member of the Triumvirate
MARCUS BRUTUS, leader of the conspiracy against Caesar
CASSIUS, instigator of the conspiracy
CASCA,
TREBONIUS,
LIGARIUS,   } conspirators against Caesar
DECIUS BRUTUS,
METELLUS CIMBER,
CINNA,
CALPURNIA, wife of Caesar
PORTIA, wife of Brutus
CICERO,
PUBLIUS,   } senators
POPILIUS LENA,
FLAVIUS, tribune
MARULLUS, tribune
CATO,
LUCILIUS,
TITINIUS,   } supporters of Brutus
MESSALA,
VOLUMNIUS,
ARTEMIDORUS, a teacher of rhetoric
CINNA, a poet
VARRO,
CLITUS,
CLAUDIUS,   } servants to Brutus
STRATO,
LUCIUS,
DARDANIUS,
PINDARUS, servant to Cassius
Ghost of Caesar
A Soothsayer
A Poet
Senators, Citizens, Soldiers, Commoners, Messengers, and Servants

SCENE: Rome, the conspirators' camp near Sardis, and the plains of Philippi.

ACT I

[SCENE I]
Rome. A Street.]

two men talk about how the people are fickle, moving from favoring Pompey to caesar

Enter Flavius, Marullus, and certain Commoners over the stage.

FLAVIUS: Hence! home, you idle creatures, get you home.
   Is this a holiday? What, know you not,
   Being mechanical, you ought not walk
   Upon a laboring day[1] without the sign
5   Of your profession? Speak, what trade art thou?
CARPENTER: Why, sir, a carpenter.
MARULLUS: Where is thy leather apron and thy rule?[2]
   What dost thou with thy best apparel on?
   You, sir, what trade are you?
10 COBBLER: Truly, sir, in respect of a fine workman, I am but, as
   you would say, a cobbler.[3]
MARULLUS: But what trade art thou? Answer me directly.
COBBLER: A trade, sir, that, I hope, I may use[4] with a safe con-
   science, which is indeed, sir, a mender of bad soles.[5]
15 MARULLUS: What trade, thou knave? Thou naughty knave,[6] what
   trade?
COBBLER: Nay, I beseech you, sir, be not out[7] with me; yet, if you
   be out, sir, I can mend you.
MARULLUS: What mean'st thou by that? Mend[8] me, thou saucy-
20   fellow!
COBBLER: Why, sir, cobble you.
FLAVIUS: Thou art a cobbler, art thou?
COBBLER: Truly, Sir, all that I live by is with the awl;[9] I meddle
   with no tradesman's matters, nor women's matters, but with
25   awl. I am indeed, sir, a surgeon to old shoes; when they are
   in great danger, I recover[10] them. As proper men as ever trod
   upon neats-leather[11] have gone upon[12] my handiwork.

[1]workday

[2]straight edge (carpenter's tool)

[3]"Cobble" means both "to imitate poorly" and "to make shoes" [The cobbler puns throughout this scene]

[4]job that I hope I may do

[5]A pun on "soles" (shoes) and "souls" (human spirits)

[6]worthless fool

[7]"upset" or "having a broken shoe"

[8]"soothe" or "repair" (as one would a shoe)

[9]the cobbler puns on "all" and "awl" (a sharp tool for punching leather) several times

[10]"save their lives" or "give them new coverings"

[11]calfskin

[12]walked in

13

FLAVIUS: But wherefore art not in thy shop today?

30   Why dost thou lead these men about the streets?

COBBLER: Truly, sir, to wear out their shoes, to get myself
    into more work. But indeed, sir, we make holiday, to see
    Caesar and to rejoice in his triumph. *massive parade celebration*

MARULLUS: Wherefore rejoice? What conquest brings he home?

35   What tributaries follow him to Rome,
    To grace in captive bonds his chariot-wheels?
    You blocks, you stones, you worse than senseless things!
    O you hard hearts, you cruel men of Rome,
    Knew you not Pompey?[13] Many a time and oft

40   Have you climb'd up to walls and battlements, *people used to*
    To towers and windows, yea, to chimney tops, *cheer for Pompey,*
    Your infants in your arms, and there have sat *now they*
    The live-long day with patient expectation *cheer*
    To see great Pompey pass the streets of Rome. *for Caesar*

45   And when you saw his chariot but appear,
    Have you not made an universal shout, *crowd, people*
    That Tiber[14] trembled underneath her banks *easily manipulated,*
    To hear the replication[15] of your sounds *change their*
    Made in her concave shores? *mind quickly*

50   And do you now put on your best attire?
    And do you now cull out[16] a holiday?
    And do you now strew flowers in his way
    That comes in triumph over Pompey's blood?
    Be gone!

55   Run to your houses, fall upon your knees,
    Pray to the gods to intermit[17] the plague
    That needs must light[18] on this ingratitude.

FLAVIUS: Go, go, good countrymen, and, for this fault,
    Assemble all the poor men of your sort,

60   Draw them to Tiber banks, and weep your tears
    Into the channel, till the lowest stream
    Do kiss the most exalted shores of all.

                              Exeunt all the Commoners.

    See, whether their basest metal[19] be not moved;
    They vanish tongue-tied in their guiltiness.

65   Go you down that way towards the Capitol;
    This way will I. Disrobe the images,
    If you do find them deck'd with ceremonies.[20]

[13]Gnaeus Pompeius Magnus, one of the rulers of Rome until Caesar defeated him at the Battle of Pharsalus, 48 B.C.

[14]the river that flows through Rome

[15]echo

[16]take for yourselves

[17]turn aside

[18]is the inevitable result

[19]deepest nature

[20]decorated for the festival

MARULLUS: May we do so?

    You know it is the feast of Lupercal.[21]

70 FLAVIUS: It is no matter; let no images

    Be hung with Caesar's trophies. I'll about,

    And drive away the vulgar[22] from the streets;

    So do you too, where you perceive them thick.[23]

    These growing feathers pluck'd from Caesar's wing

75   Will make him fly an ordinary pitch,[24]

    Who else would soar above the view of men

    And keep us all in servile fearfulness.   *Exeunt.*

(margin note: don't want people celebrating caesar)

[SCENE II

A public place.]

(margin note: Cassius speaks to Brutus about Caesar being too powerful for just a man)

Enter Caesar; Antony for the course, Calpurnia, Portia, Decius, Cicero, Brutus, Cassius, Casca; a Soothsayer; after them Marullus and Flavius.

CAESAR: Calpurnia!

CASCA: Peace, ho! Caesar speaks.

CAESAR: Calpurnia!

CALPURNIA: Here, my lord.

5 CAESAR: Stand you directly in Antonio's way,

    When he doth run his course. Antonio!

ANTONY: Caesar, my lord?

CAESAR: Forget not, in your speed, Antonio,

    To touch Calpurnia, for our elders say,

10   The barren, touched in this holy chase,[25]

    Shake off their sterile curse.

ANTONY: I shall remember.

    When Caesar says "Do this," it is perform'd.

CAESAR: Set on, and leave no ceremony out.

15 SOOTHSAYER: Caesar! *(margin note: fortune teller)*

CAESAR: Ha! Who calls?

CASCA: Bid every noise be still. Peace yet again!

CAESAR: Who is it in the press[26] that calls on me?

    I hear a tongue, shriller than all the music,

20   Cry "Caesar." Speak, Caesar is turn'd to hear.

[21]*Lupercalia, a fertility festival held in February*

[22]*common people*

[23]*see them in crowds*

[24]*at a normal height*

[25]*As part of the Lupercalia festivities, young men run naked through the streets of Rome, striking passersby with leather thongs. An infertile person struck by a thong is supposed to become fertile.*

[26]*crowd*

27 *fifteenth day
[The Roman
month was
divided into
the calends
(beginning of
the month),
ides (either the
thirteenth or
fifteenth day of
the month), and
nones (nine days
before the ides).]*

28 *have observed
you recently*

29 *used*

30 *direct my con-
cern*

31 *tarnish*

32 *ideas*

33 *except by*

SOOTHSAYER: Beware the ides of March.[27]

CAESAR: What man is that?

BRUTUS: A soothsayer bids you beware the ides of March.

CAESAR: Set him before me; let me see his face.

25 CASSIUS: Fellow, come from the throng; look upon Caesar.

CAESAR: What say'st thou to me now? Speak once again.

SOOTHSAYER: Beware the ides of March.

CAESAR: He is a dreamer; let us leave him. Pass.

                    Sennet. Exeunt [all but] Brutus and Cassius.]

CASSIUS: Will you go see the order of the course?

30 BRUTUS: Not I.

CASSIUS: I pray you, do.

BRUTUS: I am not gamesome; I do lack some part
    Of that quick spirit that is in Antony.
    Let me not hinder, Cassius, your desires;
35   I'll leave you.

CASSIUS: Brutus, I do observe you now of late;[28]
    I have not from your eyes that gentleness
    And show of love as I was wont[29] to have;
    You bear too stubborn and too strange a hand
40   Over your friend that loves you.

BRUTUS: Cassius,
    Be not deceived; if I have veil'd my look,
    I turn the trouble of my countenance[30]
    Merely upon myself. Vexed I am
45   Of late with passions of some difference,
    Conceptions only proper to myself,
    Which give some soil[31] perhaps to my behaviors;
    But let not therefore my good friends be grieved—
    Among which number, Cassius, be you one—
50   Nor construe any further my neglect
    Than that poor Brutus with himself at war
    Forgets the shows of love to other men.

CASSIUS: Then, Brutus, I have much mistook your passion,
    By means whereof this breast of mine hath buried
55   Thoughts of great value, worthy cogitations.[32]
    Tell me, good Brutus, can you see your face?

BRUTUS: No, Cassius, for the eye sees not itself
    But by[33] reflection, by some other things.

CASSIUS: 'Tis just,

60   And it is very much lamented, Brutus,
That you have no such mirrors as will turn
Your hidden worthiness into your eye
That you might see your shadow. I have heard
Where many of the best respect in Rome,

65   Except immortal Caesar, speaking of Brutus,
And groaning underneath this age's yoke,
Have wish'd that noble Brutus had his eyes.[34]

BRUTUS: Into what dangers would you lead me, Cassius,
That you would have me seek into myself

70   For that which is not in me?

CASSIUS: Therefore, good Brutus, be prepared to hear,
And since you know you cannot see yourself
So well as by reflection, I your glass
Will modestly[35] discover to yourself

75   That of yourself which you yet know not of.
And be not jealous on me, gentle Brutus;
Were I a common laugher, or did use[36]
To stale with ordinary oaths my love
To every new protester,[37] if you know

80   That I do fawn on[38] men and hug them hard
And after scandal them, or if you know
That I profess myself in banqueting
To all the rout,[39] then hold me dangerous.

Flourish, and shout.

BRUTUS: What means this shouting? I do fear the people

85   Choose Caesar for their king.

CASSIUS: Ay, do you fear it?
Then must I think you would not have it so.

BRUTUS: I would not, Cassius, yet I love him well.
But wherefore do you hold me here so long?

90   What is it that you would impart to me?
If it be aught toward the general good,
Set honor in one eye and death i' the other
And I will look on both indifferently.
For let the gods so speed me as I love[40]

95   The name of honor more than I fear death.

CASSIUS: I know that virtue to be in you, Brutus,
As well as I do know your outward favor.[41]
Well, honor is the subject of my story.

---

[34] could see himself

[35] without over-statement

[36] was accustomed

[37] applicant for friendship

[38] flatter

[39] speak too freely when I am drinking

[40] God help me

[41] appearance

[handwritten margin notes:] cassius trying to implant idea of Caesar is too powerful

Brutus says that if it is for the general good he will consider it

I cannot tell what you and other men
100   Think of this life, but, for my single self,
I had as lief not be as live to be
In awe of such a thing as I myself.
I was born free as Caesar, so were you;
We both have fed as well, and we can both
105   Endure the winter's cold as well as he.
For once, upon a raw and gusty day,
The troubled Tiber chafing[42] with her shores,
Caesar said to me, "Darest thou, Cassius, now
Leap in with me into this angry flood
110   And swim to yonder point?" Upon the word,
Accoutred[43] as I was, I plunged in
And bade him follow. So indeed he did.
The torrent roar'd, and we did buffet[44] it
With lusty sinews,[45] throwing it aside
115   And stemming it with hearts of controversy.
But ere we could arrive the point proposed,
Caesar cried, "Help me, Cassius, or I sink!"
I, as Aeneas[46] our great ancestor
Did from the flames of Troy upon his shoulder
120   The old Anchises[47] bear, so from the waves of Tiber
Did I the tired Caesar. And this man
Is now become a god, and Cassius is
A wretched creature, and must bend his body
If Caesar carelessly but nod on him.
125   He had a fever[48] when he was in Spain,
And when the fit was on him, I did mark
How he did shake. 'Tis true, this god did shake;
His coward lips did from their color fly,
And that same eye whose bend doth awe the world
130   Did lose his luster. I did hear him groan.
Ay, and that tongue of his that bade the Romans
Mark him and write his speeches in their books,
Alas, it cried, "Give me some drink, Titinius,"
As a sick girl. Ye gods! It doth amaze me
135   A man of such a feeble temper should
So get the start[49] of the majestic world
And bear the palm[50] alone.   *Shout. Flourish.*
   BRUTUS: Another general shout!

[Margin glosses:]
[42]*churning*
[43]*dressed*
[44]*beat against*
[45] *muscles*
[46]*Trojan who survived the Trojan War and came to Italy, eventually leading to the founding of Rome*
[47]*Elderly father of Aeneas, carried out of Troy on Aeneas' back*
[48]*Caesar is epileptic*
[49]*rule*
[50]*win the prize*

[Handwritten annotations:]
examples of Caesar's weaknesses
drowning
Cassius saves him
Caesar has seizures
he is not a god
he is just a man
Cassius tries to convince Brutus of this
seizures

I do believe that these applauses are
140 For some new honors that are heap'd on Caesar.
CASSIUS: Why, man, he doth bestride the narrow world
Like a Colossus,[51] and we petty men
Walk under his huge legs and peep about
To find ourselves dishonorable graves.
145 Men at some time are masters of their fates:
The fault, dear Brutus, is not in our stars,
But in ourselves, that we are underlings.
Brutus, and Caesar: what should be in that Caesar?
Why should that name be sounded more than yours?
150 Write them together, yours is as fair a name;
Sound them, it doth become the mouth as well;
Weigh them, it is as heavy; conjure with 'em,
Brutus will start a spirit as soon as Caesar.
Now, in the names of all the gods at once,
155 Upon what meat doth this our Caesar feed
That he is grown so great? Age, thou art shamed!
Rome, thou hast lost the breed of noble bloods!
When went there by an age since the great flood
But it was famed with more than with one man?
160 When could they say till now that talk'd of Rome
That her wide walls encompass'd but one man?
Now is it Rome indeed, and room enough,
When there is in it but one only man.
O, you and I have heard our fathers say
165 There was a Brutus[52] once that would have brook'd
The eternal devil to keep his state in Rome
As easily as a king.[53]
BRUTUS: That you do love me, I am nothing jealous;[54]
What you would work me to, I have some aim.[55]
170 How I have thought of this and of these times,
I shall recount hereafter; for this present,
I would not, so with love I might entreat you,[56]
Be any further moved. What you have said
I will consider; what you have to say
175 I will with patience hear, and find a time
Both meet to hear and answer such high things.
Till then, my noble friend, chew upon this:
Brutus had rather be a villager

[51]One of the Seven Wonders of the Ancient World, the Colossus was an enormous statue of Apollo said to have stood with a leg on each side of the harbor at Rhodes

[52]Lucius Junius Brutus, legendary figure who expelled the last king of Rome and established the Republic

[53]sooner allowed the devil to rule as allowed a king to rule

[54]have no doubt

[55]idea

[56]I ask you this out of love

[handwritten margin notes:] Cassius - Caesar isn't a God, he has too much power. telling Brutus he should have power

Cassius is kind of getting to Brutus - still not fully convinced - he says that he'll think about it

Than to repute himself a son of Rome

180   Under these hard conditions as this time
Is like to lay upon us.

CASSIUS: I am glad that my weak words
Have struck but thus much show of fire from Brutus.

Enter Caesar and his Train.

BRUTUS: The games are done, and Caesar is returning.

185   CASSIUS: As they pass by, pluck Casca by the sleeve,
And he will, after his sour fashion,[57] tell you
What hath proceeded worthy note[58] today.

BRUTUS: I will do so. But, look you, Cassius,
The angry spot doth glow on Caesar's brow,

190   And all the rest look like a chidden[59] train:[60]
Calpurnia's cheek is pale, and Cicero
Looks with such ferret and such fiery eyes
As we have seen him in the Capitol,
Being cross'd[61] in conference by some senators.

195   CASSIUS: Casca will tell us what the matter is.

CAESAR: Antonio!

ANTONY: Caesar?

CAESAR: Let me have men about me that are fat,
Sleek-headed men, and such as sleep o' nights:

200   Yond Cassius has a lean and hungry look;
He thinks too much; such men are dangerous.

ANTONY: Fear him not, Caesar; he's not dangerous;
He is a noble Roman and well given.

CAESAR: Would he were fatter! But I fear him not,

205   Yet if my name were liable to fear,
I do not know the man I should avoid
So soon as that spare Cassius. He reads much,
He is a great observer, and he looks
Quite through the deeds of men. He loves no plays,

210   As thou dost, Antony; he hears no music;
Seldom he smiles, and smiles in such a sort
As if he mock'd himself, and scorn'd his spirit
That could be moved to smile at any thing.
Such men as he be never at heart's ease

215   Whiles they behold a greater than themselves,
And therefore are they very dangerous.
I rather tell thee what is to be fear'd
Than what I fear, for always I am Caesar.

[57] *in his peevish way*

[58] *what has happened that is worth talking about*

[59] *scolded*

[60] *group of followers*

[61] *disagreed with*

Come on my right hand, for this ear is deaf,

220   And tell me truly what thou think'st of him.

           Sennet. Exeunt Caesar and his Train [but Casca.]

CASCA: You pull'd me by the cloak; would you speak with me?

BRUTUS: Ay, Casca, tell us what hath chanced today,

    That Caesar looks so sad.

CASCA: Why, you were with him, were you not?

225 BRUTUS: I should not then ask Casca what had chanced.

CASCA: Why, there was a crown offered him, and being offered

    him: he put it by with the back of his hand, thus, and then

    the people fell a-shouting.

BRUTUS: What was the second noise for?

230 CASCA: Why, for that too.

CASSIUS: They shouted thrice. What was the last cry for?

CASCA: Why, for that too.

BRUTUS: Was the crown offered him thrice?

CASCA: Ay, marry, wast, and he put it by thrice, every time gen-

235   tler than other, and at every putting by mine honest neigh-

    bors shouted.

CASSIUS: Who offered him the crown?

CASCA: Why, Antony.

BRUTUS: Tell us the manner of it, gentle Casca.

240 CASCA: I can as well be hang'd[62] as tell the manner of it. It was

    mere foolery; I did not mark it. I saw Mark Antony offer

    him a crown, yet 'twas not a crown neither, 'twas one of

    these coronets[63] and, as I told you, he put it by once. But for

    all that, to my thinking, he would fain have had it. Then he

245   offered it to him again; then he put it by again. But, to my

    thinking, he was very loath to lay his fingers off it. And then

    he offered it the third time; he put it the third time by; and

    still as he refused it, the rabblement hooted and clapped

    their chopped[64] hands and threw up their sweaty nightcaps

250   and uttered such a deal of stinking breath because Caesar

    refused the crown, that it had almost choked Caesar, for he

    swounded[65] and fell down at it. And for mine own part, I

    durst not laugh for fear of opening my lips and receiving the

    bad air.

255 CASSIUS: But, soft, I pray you. What, did Caesar swound?

CASCA: He fell down in the market-place and foamed at mouth

    and was speechless.

BRUTUS: 'Tis very like: he hath the falling sickness.[66]

[62]*would rather be hanged than talk about it*

[63]*ornamental crowns*

[64]*rough [indicating that they are working-class citizens]*

[65]*fell in a swoon*

[66]*epilepsy*

CASSIUS: No, Caesar hath it not, but you, and I,
260   And honest Casca, we have the falling sickness.

CASCA: I know not what you mean by that, but I am sure
Caesar fell down. If the tag-rag people did not clap him
and hiss him according as he pleased and displeased them,
as they use to do the players in the theatre, I am no true
265   man.

BRUTUS: What said he when he came unto himself?

CASCA: Marry, before he fell down, when he perceived the
common herd was glad he refused the crown, he plucked
me ope his doublet[67] and offered them his throat to cut. An
270   had been a man of any occupation,[68] if I would not have
taken him at a word, I would I might go to hell among the
rogues. And so he fell. When he came to himself again,
he said, if he had done or said any thing amiss, he desired
their worships to think it was his infirmity. Three or four
275   wenches, where I stood cried, "Alas, good soul!" and for-
gave him with all their hearts. But there's no heed to be
taken of them; if Caesar had stabbed their mothers, they
would have done no less.

BRUTUS: And after that, he came thus sad away?
280 CASCA: Ay.

CASSIUS: Did Cicero say anything?

CASCA: Ay, he spoke Greek.

CASSIUS: To what effect?

CASCA: Nay, an I tell you that, I'll ne'er look you i' the face
285   again; but those that understood him smiled at one
another and shook their heads; but for mine own part,
it was Greek to me. I could tell you more news too:
Marullus and Flavius, for pulling scarfs off Caesar's images, are put to silence. Fare you well. There was more fool-
290   ery yet, if could remember it.

CASSIUS: Will you sup with me tonight, Casca?

CASCA: No, I am promised forth.[69]

CASSIUS: Will you dine with me tomorrow?

CASCA: Ay, if I be alive, and your mind hold, and your dinner
295   worth the eating.

CASSIUS: Good, I will expect you.

CASCA: Do so, farewell, both.   *Exit.*

BRUTUS: What a blunt fellow is this grown to be!
He was quick mettle when he went to school.

---

[67] *opened his jacket*

[68] *laboring man*

[69] *I have already
made plans*

300 CASSIUS: So is he now in execution
      Of any bold or noble enterprise,
      However he puts on this tardy form.
      This rudeness is a sauce to his good wit,
      Which gives men stomach to digest his words
305   With better appetite.
    BRUTUS: And so it is. For this time I will leave you.
      Tomorrow, if you please to speak with me,
      I will come home to you, or, if you will,
      Come home to me and I will wait for you.
310 CASSIUS: I will do so. Till then, think of the world.

                                        Exit Brutus.

      Well, Brutus, thou art noble; yet, I see
      Thy honorable metal may be wrought
      From that it is disposed; therefore it is meet
      That noble minds keep ever with their likes;
315   For who so firm that cannot be seduced?
      Caesar doth bear me hard, but he loves Brutus.   *he's going to*
      If I were Brutus now and he[70] were Cassius,   *throw letters in*   [70]*Brutus*
      He should not humor[71] me. I will this night,   *his window to*   [71]*favor*
      In several hands,[72] in at his windows throw,   *make Brutus*   [72]*styles of hand-*
320   As if they came from several citizens,   *think Caesar is*   *writing*
      Writings, all tending to the great opinion   *power-hungry*
      That Rome holds of his name, wherein obscurely[73]   [73]*indirectly*
      Caesar's ambition shall be glanced at.[74]   [74]*hinted at*
      And after this let Caesar seat him sure;
325   For we will shake him, or worse days endure.

                  Cassius - wanting to shake caesar up   *Exit.*

Casca - words look longer, indicate
lower class; not all conspirators are
upper class
Brutus & Cassius - words look like poetry

[SCENE III
A street.]

[handwritten: Cassius manipulating Casca to join him against Caesar. Cinna comes and told to deliver fake letters to Brutus]

[handwritten: Storm- something bad is happening; things not under control]

Thunder and lightning. Enter Casca, and Cicero.

CICERO: Good even, Casca. Brought you Caesar home?
 Why are you breathless, and why stare you so?
CASCA: Are not you moved, when all the sway[75] of earth
 Shakes like a thing unfirm? O Cicero,
5 I have seen tempests, when the scolding winds
 Have rived[76] the knotty oaks, and I have seen
 The ambitious ocean swell and rage and foam,
 To be exalted[77] with the threatening clouds,
 But never till tonight, never till now,
10 Did I go through a tempest dropping fire. *[handwritten: casca feeling many bad signs, fearful]*
 Either there is a civil strife in heaven,
 Or else the world too saucy with the gods
 Incenses them[78] to send destruction.
CICERO: Why, saw you anything more wonderful?
15 CASCA: A common slave—you know him well by sight—
 Held up his left hand, which did flame and burn
 Like twenty torches join'd, and yet his hand,
 Not sensible[79] of fire, remain'd unscorch'd.
 Besides—I ha' not since put up my sword—
20 Against the Capitol I met a lion,
 Who glazed[80] upon me and went surly by
 Without annoying me: and there were drawn
 Upon a heap[81] a hundred ghastly[82] women
 Transformed with their fear, who swore they saw
25 Men all in fire walk up and down the streets.
 And yesterday the bird of night[83] did sit
 Even at noon-day upon the market-place,
 Howling and shrieking. When these prodigies[84]
30 Do so conjointly[85] meet, let not men say
 "These are their reasons; they are natural,"
 For, I believe, they are portentous[86] things
 Unto the climate that they point upon.
CICERO: Indeed, it is a strange-disposed time;
35 But men may construe things after their fashion,

[75]natural order

[76]split

[77]lifted up

[78]makes them angry enough

[79]showing evidence of

[80]gazed

[81]gathered in a crowd

[82]pale with fright

[83]owl

[84]strange signs

[85]at the same time

[86]significant

Clean from the purpose of the things themselves.[87]
Come Caesar to the Capitol tomorrow?

CASCA: He doth; for he did bid Antonius
    Send word to you he would be there tomorrow.

40 CICERO: Good then, Casca. This disturbed sky
    Is not to walk in.

CASCA: Farewell, Cicero.   *Exit*
    Cicero.

45 *Enter Cassius.*

CASSIUS: Who's there?

CASCA: A Roman.

CASSIUS: Casca, by your voice.

50 CASCA: Your ear is good. Cassius, what night is this!

CASSIUS: A very pleasing night to honest men.

CASCA: Who ever knew the heavens menace so?

CASSIUS: Those that have known the earth so full of faults.
    For my part, I have walk'd about the streets,
55   Submitting me unto the perilous night,
    And thus unbraced,[88] Casca, as you see,
    Have bared my bosom to the thunder-stone;[89]
    And when the cross blue lightning seem'd to open
    The breast of heaven, I did present myself
60   Even in the aim and very flash of it.

CASCA: But wherefore did you so much tempt the heavens?
    It is the part of men to fear and tremble
    When the most mighty gods by tokens send
    Such dreadful heralds to astonish us.

CASSIUS: You are dull, Casca, and those sparks of life
65   That should be in a Roman you do want,
    Or else you use not. You look pale and gaze
    And put on fear and cast yourself in wonder,
    To see the strange impatience of the heavens.
    But if you would consider the true cause
70   Why all these fires, why all these gliding ghosts,
    Why birds and beasts from quality and kind,[90]
    Why old men fool, and children calculate,[91]
    Why all these things change from their ordinance,[92]
    Their natures and preformed faculties,
    To monstrous quality, why, you shall find

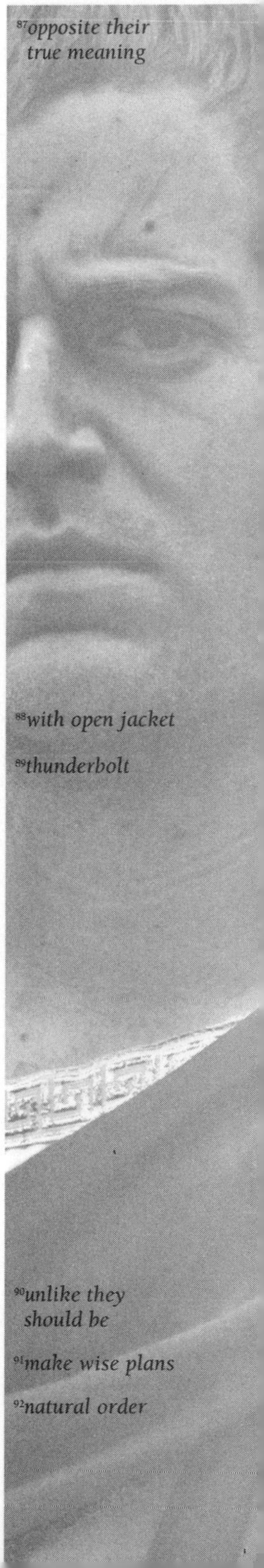

[87] opposite their true meaning

[88] with open jacket

[89] thunderbolt

[90] unlike they should be

[91] make wise plans

[92] natural order

[handwritten margin note: Cassius reinterprets signs and turns Casca to his side against Caesar]

75   That heaven hath infused them with these spirits
        To make them instruments of fear and warning
        Unto some monstrous state.
        Now could I, Casca, name to thee a man
        Most like this dreadful night,
80   That thunders, lightens, opens graves, and roars
        As doth the lion in the Capitol,
        A man no mightier than thyself or me
        In personal action, yet prodigious[93] grown
        And fearful, as these strange eruptions are.
85 CASCA: 'Tis Caesar that you mean, is it not, Cassius?
    CASSIUS: Let it be who it is, for Romans now
        Have thews[94] and limbs like to their ancestors.
        But, woe the while! Our fathers' minds are dead,
        And we are govern'd with our mothers' spirits;
90   Our yoke and sufferance show us womanish.
    CASCA: Indeed they say the senators tomorrow
        Mean to establish Caesar as a king,
        And he shall wear his crown by sea and land,
        In every place save here in Italy.
95 CASSIUS: I know where I will wear this dagger then:
        Cassius from bondage will deliver Cassius.
        Therein, ye gods, you make the weak most strong;
        Therein, ye gods, you tyrants do defeat.
        Nor stony tower, nor walls of beaten brass,
100   Nor airless dungeon, nor strong links of iron,
        Can be retentive to[95] the strength of spirit;
        But life, being weary of these worldly bars,
        Never lacks power to dismiss itself.
        If I know this, know all the world besides,
105   That part of tyranny that I do bear
        I can shake off at pleasure.   *Thunder still.*
    CASCA: So can I.
        So every bondman[96] in his own hand bears
        The power to cancel his captivity.
110 CASSIUS: And why should Caesar be a tyrant then?
        Poor man! I know he would not be a wolf
        But that he sees the Romans are but sheep.
        He were no lion, were not Romans hinds.
        Those that with haste will make a mighty fire

[93]*unusual*

[94]*muscles*

[95]*hold back*

[96]*servant*

115 Begin it with weak straws. What trash is Rome,
     What rubbish and what offal, when it serves
     For the base matter to illuminate
     So vile a thing as Caesar? But, O grief,
     Where hast thou led me? I perhaps speak this

     [handwritten: 119 oops, I'm not sure if I can trust you. I've said all these things]

120 Before a willing bondman; then I know
     My answer must be made.[97] But I am arm'd,
     And dangers are to me indifferent.
   CASCA: You speak to Casca, and to such a man   *[handwritten: make a deal]*
     That is no fleering[98] tell-tale. Hold, my hand.
125 Be factious[99] for redress of all these griefs,   *[handwritten: – make a faction,]*
     And I will set this foot of mine as far   *[handwritten: group against Caesar]*
     As who goes farthest.
   CASSIUS: There's a bargain made.
     Now know you, Casca, I have moved already
130 Some certain of the noblest-minded Romans
     To undergo with me an enterprise
     Of honorable-dangerous consequence;
     And I do know, by this they stay for me
     In Pompey's Porch.[100] For now, this fearful night,
135 There is no stir or walking in the streets,
     And the complexion[101] of the element
     In favor's like the work we have in hand,
     Most bloody, fiery, and most terrible.

     Enter Cinna.

   CASCA: Stand close awhile, for here comes one in haste.
140 CASSIUS: 'Tis Cinna, I do know him by his gait;
     He is a friend. Cinna, where haste you so?
   CINNA: To find out you. Who's that? Metellus Cimber?
   CASSIUS: No, it is Casca, one incorporate[102]
     To our attempts. Am I not stay'd for, Cinna?
145 CINNA: I am glad on't. What a fearful night is this!
     There's two or three of us have seen strange sights.
   CASSIUS: Am I not stay'd for? Tell me.   *[handwritten: need Brutus to join them because the people see Brutus as honorable, trust him]*
   CINNA: Yes, you are.
     O Cassius, if you could
150 But win the noble Brutus to our party—
   CASSIUS: Be you content. Good Cinna, take this paper,   *[handwritten: trying to convince Brutus]*

[97]*I will suffer the consequences*

[98]*flattering*

[99]*forming a faction or party*

[100]*porch outside the Theater of Pompey, on a plain next to the Tiber*

[101]*nature*

[102]*willing to cooperate with*

[103]*chair of the second-highest ranking official in the Senate (Brutus currently holds the seat)*

[104]*the figure from Roman history mentioned earlier*

[105]*transformation of lead into gold*

[106]*gotten the idea of*

And look you lay it in the praetor's[103] chair,
Where Brutus may but find it; and throw this
In at his window; set this up with wax
155   Upon old Brutus'[104] statue. All this done,
Repair to Pompey's porch, where you shall find us.
Is Decius Brutus and Trebonius there?
CINNA: All but Metellus Cimber, and he's gone
To seek you at your house. Well, I will hie
160   And so bestow these papers as you bade me.
CASSIUS: That done, repair to Pompey's theatre.

Exit Cinna.

Come, Casca, you and I will yet ere day
See Brutus at his house. Three parts of him
Is ours already, and the man entire
165   Upon the next encounter yields him ours.
CASCA: O, he sits high in all the people's hearts,
And that which would appear offense in us,
His countenance, like richest alchemy,[105]
Will change to virtue and to worthiness.
170   CASSIUS: Him and his worth and our great need of him
You have right well conceited.[106] Let us go,
For it is after midnight, and ere day
We will awake him and be sure of him.

Exeunt.

Cassius manipulating
Casca, Brutus ←
storm — not very good minny

ACT II

[SCENE 1]

Brutus receives fake letters, believes them. Other conspirators come and Brutus takes control of the group. Portia is worried, Caius Ligarius comes and tells that he will follow Brutus w/o reason.

Enter Brutus in his orchard.

BRUTUS: *[Calling out.]* What, Lucius, ho!
    I cannot, by the progress of the stars,
    Gives guess how near to day. Lucius, I say!
    I would it were my fault to sleep so soundly.
5   When, Lucius, when? awake, I say! what, Lucius!

Enter Lucius.

LUCIUS: Call'd you, my lord?
BRUTUS: Get me a taper[1] in my study, Lucius.   [1]candle
    When it is lighted, come and call me here.
LUCIUS: I will, my lord.   *Exit.*
10 BRUTUS: It must be by his death, and, for my part,
    I know no personal cause to spurn at him,
    But for the general.[2] He would be crown'd: [2]general good
    How that might change his nature, there's the question.
    It is the bright day that brings forth the adder[3]   [3]poisonous snake
15   And that craves[4] wary[5] walking. Crown him? that;   [4]calls for
    And then, I grant, we put a sting in him   [5]careful
    That at his will he may do danger with.
    The abuse of greatness is when it disjoins
    Remorse from power, and, to speak truth of Caesar,
20   I have not known when his affections sway'd
    More than his reason. But 'tis a common proof[6]   [6]generally
    That lowliness is young ambition's ladder,   accepted fact
    Whereto the climber-upward turns his face;
    But when he once attains the upmost round,
25   He then unto the ladder turns his back,

Looks in the clouds, scorning the base degrees
By which he did ascend. So Caesar may;
Then, lest he may, prevent. And, since the quarrel
Will bear no color for the thing he is,[7]
30   Fashion it thus, that what he is, augmented,[8]
Would run to these and these extremities;
And therefore think him as a serpent's egg
Which hatch'd would as his kind grow mischievous,
And kill him in the shell.

[Re-]enter Lucius with a taper.

35   LUCIUS: The taper burneth in your closet, sir.
Searching the window for a flint[9] I found
This paper thus seal'd up, and I am sure
It did not lie there when I went to bed.

Gives him the letter.

BRUTUS: Get you to bed again, it is not day.
40   Is not tomorrow, boy, the ides of March?
LUCIUS: I know not, sir.
BRUTUS: Look in the calendar and bring me word.
LUCIUS: I will, sir.   *Exit.*
BRUTUS: The exhalations[10] whizzing in the air
45   Give so much light that I may read by them.

Opens the letter, and reads.

"Brutus, thou sleep'st: awake and see thyself!
Shall Rome, &c. Speak, strike, redress!"[11]
"Brutus, thou sleep'st: awake!"

Such instigations[12] have been often dropp'd
50   Where I have took them up.
"Shall Rome, &c." Thus must I piece it out.
Shall Rome stand under one man's awe? What, Rome?
My ancestors did from the streets of Rome
The Tarquin[13] drive, when he was call'd a king.
55   "Speak, strike, redress!" Am I entreated
To speak and strike? O Rome, I make thee promise,
If the redress will follow,[14] thou receivest
Thy full petition[15] at the hand of Brutus!

[7][because there is no reason to criticize him yet]

[8]his nature, if power is added to it

[9]lighter for the candle

[10]meteors

[11]avenge

[12]attempts to start a rebellion

[13]Tarquin, the tyrannical last king of Rome [driven out by Lucius Junius Brutus]

[14]if what is wrong will be made right

[15]everything you want

[Re-]enter Lucius.

LUCIUS: Sir, March is wasted fifteen days.

Knocking within.

60 BRUTUS: 'Tis good. Go to the gate, somebody knocks.

Exit Lucius.

Since Cassius first did whet[16] me against Caesar
I have not slept.
Between the acting of a dreadful thing
And the first motion,[17] all the interim is
65 Like a phantasma or a hideous dream;
The genius[18] and the mortal instruments[19]
Are then in council,[20] and the state of man,
Like to a little kingdom, suffers then
The nature of an insurrection.

[Re-]Enter Lucius.[with a taper.]

70 LUCIUS: Sir, 'tis your brother Cassius at the door,
　　Who doth desire to see you.
BRUTUS:　　　　　　Is he alone?
LUCIUS: No, sir, there are moe with him.

BRUTUS:　　　　　　　Do you know them?
75 LUCIUS: No, sir, their hats are pluck'd[21] about their ears,
　　And half their faces buried in their cloaks,
　　That by no means I may discover them
　　By any mark of favor.[22]
BRUTUS:　　　　　Let 'em enter.　　*[Exit Lucius.]*
80 They are the faction. O Conspiracy,
Shamest thou to show thy dangerous brow by night,
When evils are most free? O, then, by day
Where wilt thou find a cavern dark enough
To mask thy monstrous visage?[23] Seek none, conspiracy;
85 Hide it in smiles and affability;
For if thou path,[24] thy native semblance[25] on,
Not Erebus[26] itself were dim enough
To hide thee from prevention.

16 sharpen

17 first idea

18 nature

19 intellect and emotion

20 debating

21 pulled down

22 outward characteristic

23 face

24 go forward

25 undisguised nature

26 in classical mythology, the dark region through which souls must pass before reaching Hades

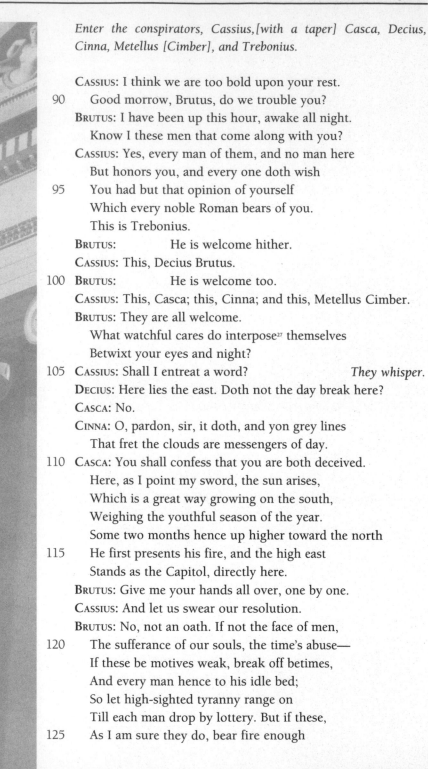

Enter the conspirators, Cassius,[with a taper] Casca, Decius, Cinna, Metellus [Cimber], and Trebonius.

CASSIUS: I think we are too bold upon your rest.
90   Good morrow, Brutus, do we trouble you?
BRUTUS: I have been up this hour, awake all night.
    Know I these men that come along with you?
CASSIUS: Yes, every man of them, and no man here
    But honors you, and every one doth wish
95   You had but that opinion of yourself
    Which every noble Roman bears of you.
    This is Trebonius.
BRUTUS: He is welcome hither.
CASSIUS: This, Decius Brutus.
100 BRUTUS: He is welcome too.
CASSIUS: This, Casca; this, Cinna; and this, Metellus Cimber.
BRUTUS: They are all welcome.
    What watchful cares do interpose[27] themselves
    Betwixt your eyes and night?
105 CASSIUS: Shall I entreat a word?   *They whisper.*
DECIUS: Here lies the east. Doth not the day break here?
CASCA: No.
CINNA: O, pardon, sir, it doth, and yon grey lines
    That fret the clouds are messengers of day.
110 CASCA: You shall confess that you are both deceived.
    Here, as I point my sword, the sun arises,
    Which is a great way growing on the south,
    Weighing the youthful season of the year.
    Some two months hence up higher toward the north
115   He first presents his fire, and the high east
    Stands as the Capitol, directly here.
BRUTUS: Give me your hands all over, one by one.
CASSIUS: And let us swear our resolution.
BRUTUS: No, not an oath. If not the face of men,
120   The sufferance of our souls, the time's abuse—
    If these be motives weak, break off betimes,
    And every man hence to his idle bed;
    So let high-sighted tyranny range on
    Till each man drop by lottery. But if these,
125   As I am sure they do, bear fire enough

[27] *place*

To kindle cowards and to steel with valor
The melting spirits of women, then, countrymen,
What need we any spur but our own cause
To prick us to redress? What other bond

130 Than secret Romans that have spoke the word
And will not palter?²⁸ And what other oath
Than honesty to honesty engaged
That this shall be or we will fall for it?
Swear priests and cowards and men cautelous,²⁹

135 Old feeble carrions³⁰ and such suffering souls
That welcome wrongs; unto bad causes swear
Such creatures as men doubt; but do not stain
The even virtue of our enterprise,
Nor the insuppressive³¹ mettle of our spirits,

140 To think that or our cause or our performance
Did need an oath; when every drop of blood
That every Roman bears, and nobly bears,
Is guilty of a several bastardy
If he do break the smallest particle

145 Of any promise that hath pass'd from him.

CASSIUS: But what of Cicero? Shall we sound him?
    I think he will stand very strong with us.

CASCA: Let us not leave him out.

CINNA: No, by no means.

150 METELLUS: O, let us have him, for his silver hairs
    Will purchase us a good opinion,
    And buy men's voices to commend our deeds.
    It shall be said his judgement ruled our hands;
    Our youths and wildness shall no whit appear,

155 But all be buried in his gravity.

BRUTUS: O, name him not; let us not break with³² him,
    For he will never follow anything
    That other men begin.

CASSIUS: Then leave him out.

160 CASCA: Indeed he is not fit.

DECIUS: Shall no man else be touch'd but only Caesar?

CASSIUS: Decius, well urged. I think it is not meet
    Mark Antony, so well beloved of Caesar,
    Should outlive Caesar. We shall find of him

165 A shrewd contriver; and you know his means,

²⁸be weak

²⁹deceitful

³⁰carcasses

³¹invincible

³²break our secret to

[handwritten margin notes: making long speech, taking control, leadership of faction]

[handwritten margin notes: Decius & Cassius want to kill Antony]

If he improve them, may well stretch so far
As to annoy us all, which to prevent,
Let Antony and Caesar fall together.

BRUTUS: Our course will seem too bloody, Caius Cassius,
170 To cut the head off and then hack the limbs
Like wrath in death and envy[33] afterwards;
For Antony is but a limb of Caesar.
Let us be sacrificers, but not butchers, Caius.
We all stand up against the spirit of Caesar,
175 And in the spirit of men there is no blood.
O, that we then could come by Caesar's spirit,
And not dismember Caesar! But, alas,
Caesar must bleed for it! And, gentle friends,
Let's kill him boldly, but not wrathfully;
180 Let's carve him as a dish fit for the gods,
Not hew him as a carcass fit for hounds;
And let our hearts, as subtle masters do,
Stir up their servants to an act of rage
And after seem to chide 'em. This shall make
185 Our purpose necessary and not envious,
Which so appearing to the common eyes,
We shall be call'd purgers, not murderers.
And for Mark Antony, think not of him,
For he can do no more than Caesar's arm
190 When Caesar's head is off.

CASSIUS: Yet I fear him,
For in the ingrafted[34] love he bears to Caesar—

BRUTUS: Alas, good Cassius, do not think of him.
If he love Caesar, all that he can do
195 Is to himself, take thought and die for Caesar.[35]
And that were much[36] he should, for he is given
To sports, to wildness, and much company.

TREBONIUS: There is no fear[37] in him, let him not die,
For he will live and laugh at this hereafter.   *Clock strikes.*[38]

200 BRUTUS: Peace, count the clock.

CASSIUS: The clock hath stricken three.

TREBONIUS: 'Tis time to part.

CASSIUS: But it is doubtful yet
Whether Caesar will come forth today or no,
205 For he is superstitious grown of late,

[33]*spitefulness*

[34]*deep-rooted*

[35]*die of grief for Caesar*

[36]*much to expect*

[37]*nothing to be afraid of*

[38]*the clock is an anachronism*

Quite from the main opinion[39] he held once
Of fantasy, of dreams and ceremonies.
It may be these apparent prodigies,[40]
The unaccustom'd[41] terror of this night,
210 And the persuasion of his augurers[42]
May hold him from the Capitol today.
DECIUS: Never fear that. If he be so resolved,
I can o'ersway[43] him, for he loves to hear
That unicorns may be betray'd[44] with trees,[45]
215 And bears with glasses, elephants with holes,
Lions with toils, and men with flatterers;
But when I tell him he hates flatterers,
He says he does, being then most flattered.
Let me work;
220 For I can give his humor the true bent,[46]
And I will bring him to the Capitol.
CASSIUS: Nay, we will all of us be there to fetch him.
BRUTUS: By the eighth hour. Is that the uttermost?
CINNA: Be that the uttermost, and fail not then.
225 METELLUS: Caius Ligarius doth bear Caesar hard,
Who rated him for speaking well of Pompey.
I wonder none of you have thought of him.
BRUTUS: Now, good Metellus, go along by him.
He loves me well, and I have given him reasons;
230 Send him but hither, and I'll fashion him.
CASSIUS: The morning comes upon's. We'll leave you, Brutus,
And, friends, disperse yourselves, but all remember
What you have said and show yourselves true Romans.
BRUTUS: Good gentlemen, look fresh and merrily;
235 Let not our looks put on our purposes,
But bear it as our Roman actors do,
With untired spirits and formal constancy.[47]
And so, good morrow to you every one.

Exeunt [all but] Brutus.

Boy! Lucius! Fast asleep? It is no matter.
240 Enjoy the honey-heavy dew of slumber;
Thou hast no figures nor no fantasies,
Which busy care draws in the brains of men;
Therefore thou sleep'st so sound.

[39]*contrary to the firm belief*

[40]*signs*

[41]*unusual*

[42]*fortune-tellers*

[43]*overcome*

[44]*captured*

[45]*[because their horns get stuck]*

[46]*bring out his true nature*

[47]*fitting dignity*

Enter Portia.

PORTIA: Brutus, my lord!

245   BRUTUS: Portia, what mean you? Wherefore rise you now?
         It is not for your health thus to commit
         Your weak condition to the raw cold morning.
      PORTIA: Nor for yours neither. Y'have ungently,[48] Brutus,
         Stole from my bed; and yesternight at supper
250   You suddenly arose and walk'd about,
         Musing and sighing, with your arms across;
         And when I ask'd you what the matter was,
         You stared upon me with ungentle looks.
         I urged you further; then you scratch'd your head,
255   And too impatiently stamp'd with your foot.
         Yet I insisted, yet you answer'd not,
         But with an angry wafture[49] of your hand
         Gave sign for me to leave you. So I did,
         Fearing to strengthen that impatience
260   Which seem'd too much enkindled,[50] and withal
         Hoping it was but an effect of humor,
         Which sometime hath his hour with every man.
         It will not let you eat, nor talk, nor sleep,
         And, could it work so much upon your shape
265   As it hath much prevail'd on your condition,[51]
         I should not know you, Brutus. Dear my lord,
         Make me acquainted with your cause of grief.
      BRUTUS: I am not well in health, and that is all.
      PORTIA: Brutus is wise, and, were he not in health,
270   He would embrace the means to come by it.
      BRUTUS: Why, so I do. Good Portia, go to bed.
      PORTIA: Is Brutus sick, and is it physical[52]
         To walk unbraced and suck up the humors
         Of the dank morning? What, is Brutus sick,
275   And will he steal out of his wholesome bed
         To dare the vile contagion of the night
         And tempt the rheumy and unpurged[53] air
         To add unto his sickness? No, my Brutus,
         You have some sick offense within your mind,
280   Which by the right and virtue of my place

[48]*unkindly*

[49]*shake*

[50]*stirred up*

[51]*if it changed your body as it has your personality*

[52]*healthy*

[53]*unclean*

[handwritten note: Portia asking whats going on]

      I ought to know of; and, upon my knees,
      I charm you, by my once commended beauty,
      By all your vows of love and that great vow
      Which did incorporate and make us one,
285   That you unfold to me, yourself, your half,
      Why you are heavy, and what men tonight
      Have had resort to you; for here have been
      Some six or seven, who did hide their faces
      Even from darkness.
290 BRUTUS: Kneel not, gentle Portia.
     PORTIA: I should not need, if you were gentle Brutus.
      Within the bond of marriage, tell me, Brutus,
      Is it excepted I should know no secrets
      That appertain to you? Am I yourself
295   But, as it were, in sort or limitation,
      To keep with you at meals, comfort your bed,
      And talk to you sometimes? Dwell I but in the suburbs
      Of your good pleasure? If it be no more,
      Portia is Brutus' harlot, not his wife.
300 BRUTUS: You are my true and honorable wife,
      As dear to me as are the ruddy drops
      That visit my sad heart.
     PORTIA: If this were true, then should I know this secret.
      I grant I am a woman, but withal
305   A woman that Lord Brutus took to wife.
      I grant I am a woman, but withal
      A woman well reputed, Cato's daughter.
      Think you I am no stronger than my sex,
      Being so father'd and so husbanded?
310   Tell me your counsels, I will not disclose em.
      I have made strong proof of my constancy,
      Giving myself a voluntary wound[54]
      Here in the thigh. Can I bear that with patience
      And not my husband's secrets?
315 BRUTUS: O ye gods,
      Render me worthy of this noble wife!   *Knock [within.]*
      Hark, hark, one knocks. Portia, go in awhile,
      And by and by thy bosom shall partake
      The secrets of my heart.
320   All my engagements I will construe[55] to thee,

[54] *Portia stabs herself*

[55] *lay out*

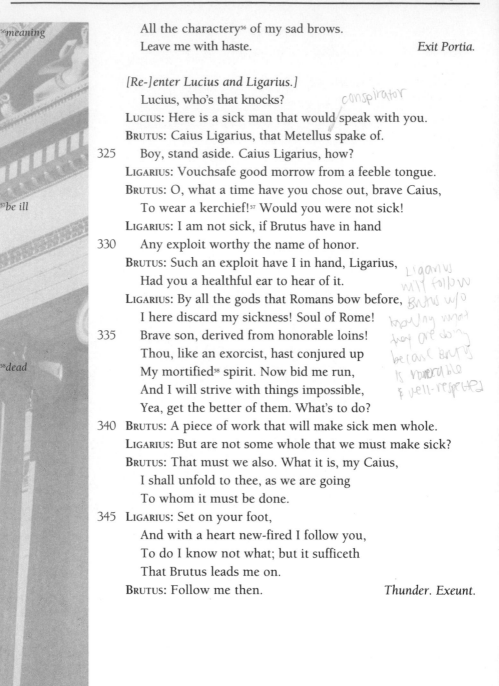

All the charactery[56] of my sad brows.
Leave me with haste.   *Exit Portia.*

[Re-]enter Lucius and Ligarius.]
    Lucius, who's that knocks?
LUCIUS: Here is a sick man that would speak with you.
BRUTUS: Caius Ligarius, that Metellus spake of.
325   Boy, stand aside. Caius Ligarius, how?
LIGARIUS: Vouchsafe good morrow from a feeble tongue.
BRUTUS: O, what a time have you chose out, brave Caius,
    To wear a kerchief![57] Would you were not sick!
LIGARIUS: I am not sick, if Brutus have in hand
330   Any exploit worthy the name of honor.
BRUTUS: Such an exploit have I in hand, Ligarius,
    Had you a healthful ear to hear of it.
LIGARIUS: By all the gods that Romans bow before,
    I here discard my sickness! Soul of Rome!
335   Brave son, derived from honorable loins!
    Thou, like an exorcist, hast conjured up
    My mortified[58] spirit. Now bid me run,
    And I will strive with things impossible,
    Yea, get the better of them. What's to do?
340 BRUTUS: A piece of work that will make sick men whole.
LIGARIUS: But are not some whole that we must make sick?
BRUTUS: That must we also. What it is, my Caius,
    I shall unfold to thee, as we are going
    To whom it must be done.
345 LIGARIUS: Set on your foot,
    And with a heart new-fired I follow you,
    To do I know not what; but it sufficeth
    That Brutus leads me on.
BRUTUS: Follow me then.   *Thunder. Exeunt.*

[56] *meaning*

[57] *be ill*

[58] *dead*

[SCENE II
Caesar's house.]

[handwritten: Calpurnia tries to convince Caesar to stay home. Decius, a conspirator, comes and convinces Caesar to go to the senate.]

Thunder and lightning. Enter Caesar, in his night-gown.

CAESAR: Nor heaven nor earth have been at peace tonight.
   Thrice hath Calpurnia in her sleep cried out,
   "Help, ho! They murder Caesar!" Who's within?

Enter a Servant.

SERVANT: My lord?
5 CAESAR: Go bid the priests do present sacrifice,
   And bring me their opinions of success.[59]
   SERVANT: I will, my lord.   *Exit.*

Enter Calpurnia.

[59]*these would come by interpreting the entrails of the sacrificed animals*

CALPURNIA: What mean you, Caesar? Think you to walk forth?
   You shall not stir out of your house today.
10 CAESAR: Caesar shall forth: the things that threaten'd me
   Ne'er look'd but on my back; when they shall see
   The face of Caesar, they are vanished.
   CALPURNIA: Caesar, I never stood on ceremonies,
   Yet now they fright me. There is one within,
15   Besides the things that we have heard and seen,
   Recounts most horrid sights seen by the watch.
   A lioness hath whelped in the streets;
   And graves have yawn'd, and yielded up their dead;
   Fierce fiery warriors fight upon the clouds,
20   In ranks and squadrons and right form of war,
   Which drizzled blood upon the Capitol;
   The noise of battle hurtled in the air,
   Horses did neigh and dying men did groan,
   And ghosts did shriek and squeal about the streets.
25   O Caesar! These things are beyond all use,
   And I do fear them.
   CAESAR: What can be avoided
   Whose end is purposed by the mighty gods?
   Yet Caesar shall go forth, for these predictions

[handwritten: Calpurnia wants Caesar to stay home]

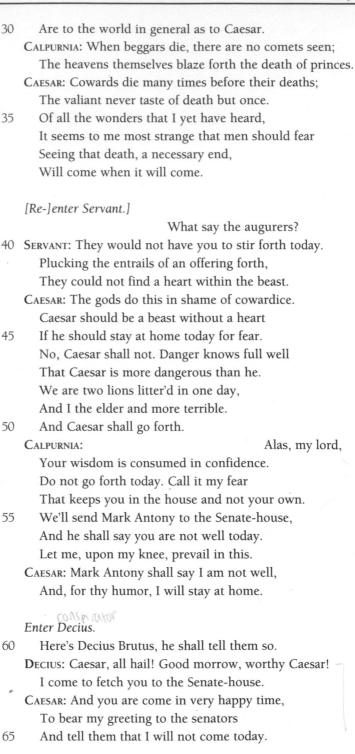

30   Are to the world in general as to Caesar.

CALPURNIA: When beggars die, there are no comets seen;
    The heavens themselves blaze forth the death of princes.

CAESAR: Cowards die many times before their deaths;
    The valiant never taste of death but once.

35   Of all the wonders that I yet have heard,
    It seems to me most strange that men should fear
    Seeing that death, a necessary end,
    Will come when it will come.

[Re-]enter Servant.]

                       What say the augurers?

40   SERVANT: They would not have you to stir forth today.
    Plucking the entrails of an offering forth,
    They could not find a heart within the beast.

CAESAR: The gods do this in shame of cowardice.
    Caesar should be a beast without a heart

45   If he should stay at home today for fear.
    No, Caesar shall not. Danger knows full well
    That Caesar is more dangerous than he.
    We are two lions litter'd in one day,
    And I the elder and more terrible.

50   And Caesar shall go forth.

CALPURNIA: Alas, my lord,
    Your wisdom is consumed in confidence.
    Do not go forth today. Call it my fear
    That keeps you in the house and not your own.

55   We'll send Mark Antony to the Senate-house,
    And he shall say you are not well today.
    Let me, upon my knee, prevail in this.

CAESAR: Mark Antony shall say I am not well,
    And, for thy humor, I will stay at home.

Enter Decius. conspirator

60   Here's Decius Brutus, he shall tell them so.

DECIUS: Caesar, all hail! Good morrow, worthy Caesar!
    I come to fetch you to the Senate-house.

CAESAR: And you are come in very happy time,
    To bear my greeting to the senators

65   And tell them that I will not come today.

Cannot, is false, and that I dare not, falser:
I will not come today. Tell them so, Decius.
CALPURNIA: Say he is sick.
CAESAR: Shall Caesar send a lie?
70 Have I in conquest stretch'd mine arm so far
To be afeard to tell greybeards the truth?
Decius, go tell them Caesar will not come.
DECIUS: Most mighty Caesar, let me know some cause,
Lest I be laugh'd at when I tell them so.
75 CAESAR: The cause is in my will: I will not come,
That is enough to satisfy the Senate.
But, for your private satisfaction,
Because I love you, I will let you know.
Calpurnia here, my wife, stays me at home;
80 She dreamt tonight she saw my statue,
Which like a fountain with an hundred spouts,
Did run pure blood, and many lusty Romans
Came smiling and did bathe their hands in it.
And these does she apply for warnings and portents
85 And evils imminent, and on her knee
Hath begg'd that I will stay at home today.
DECIUS: This dream is all amiss interpreted;
It was a vision fair and fortunate.
Your statue spouting blood in many pipes,
90 In which so many smiling Romans bathed,
Signifies that from you great Rome shall suck
Reviving blood, and that great men shall press
For tinctures, stains, relics, and cognizance.[60]
This by Calpurnia's dream is signified.
95 CAESAR: And this way have you well expounded it.
DECIUS: I have, when you have heard what I can say.
And know it now, the Senate have concluded
To give this day a crown to mighty Caesar.
If you shall send them word you will not come,
100 Their minds may change. Besides, it were a mock
Apt to be render'd,[61] for some one to say
"Break up the Senate till another time,
When Caesar's wife shall meet with better dreams."
If Caesar hide himself, shall they not whisper
105 "Lo, Caesar is afraid"?

[60]*souvenirs bearing the blood of Caesar*

[61]*likely to be made*

Pardon me, Caesar, for my dear dear love
To your proceeding bids me tell you this,
And reason to my love is liable.

CAESAR: How foolish do your fears seem now, Calpurnia!
110   I am ashamed I did yield to them.
Give me my robe, for I will go.

Enter Brutus, Ligarius, Metellus [Cimber], Casca, Trebonius, Cinna, and Publius.

And look where Publius is come to fetch me.

PUBLIUS: Good morrow, Caesar.

CAESAR: Welcome, Publius.
115   What, Brutus, are you stirr'd so early too?
Good morrow, Casca. Caius Ligarius,
    Caesar was ne'er so much your enemy
    As that same ague which hath made you lean.
What is't o'clock?
120 BRUTUS: Caesar, 'tis strucken eight.

CAESAR: I thank you for your pains and courtesy.

Enter Antony.

    See, Antony, that revels long o' nights,
    Is notwithstanding[62] up. Good morrow, Antony.

ANTONY: So to most noble Caesar.
125 CAESAR: Bid them prepare within.
    I am to blame to be thus waited for.
    Now, Cinna; now, Metellus; what, Trebonius,
    I have an hour's talk in store for you;
    Remember that you call on me today;
130   Be near me, that I may remember you.

TREBONIUS: Caesar, I will. And so near will I be
    That your best friends shall wish I had been further.

CAESAR: Good friends, go in and taste some wine with me,
    And we like friends will straightway go together.
135 BRUTUS: That every like is not the same, O Caesar,
    The heart of Brutus yearns to think upon!

Exeunt.

[62]*nevertheless*

[SCENE III
A street near the Capitol.]

Enter Artemidorus, [reading paper.]

ARTEMIDORUS: "Caesar, beware of Brutus; take heed of Cassius;
come not near Casca; have an eye to Cinna; trust not
Trebonius; mark it well Metellus Cimber; Decius Brutus
loves thee not; thou hast wronged Caius Ligarius. There is
5　　but one mind in all these men, and it is bent against Caesar.
If thou beest not immortal, look about you. Security gives
way to conspiracy. The mighty gods defend thee!
　　　　　　　　Thy lover, Artemidorus."
Here will I stand till Caesar pass along,
10　And as a suitor will I give him this.
My heart laments that virtue cannot live
Out of the teeth of emulation.
If thou read this, O Caesar, thou mayest live;
If not, the Fates with traitors do contrive.　　　　*Exit.*

[SCENE IV
Another part of the same street,
before the house of Brutus.]

Enter Portia and Lucius.

PORTIA: I prithee, boy, run to the Senate-house;
Stay not to answer me, but get thee gone.
Why dost thou stay?
LUCIUS:　　　　　　To know my errand, madam.
5　PORTIA: I would have had thee there, and here again,
Ere I can tell thee what thou shouldst do there.
O constancy, be strong upon my side!
Set a huge mountain 'tween my heart and tongue!
I have a man's mind, but a woman's might.
10　How hard it is for women to keep counsel![63]
Art thou here yet?
LUCIUS:　　　　　　Madam, what should I do?
Run to the Capitol, and nothing else?
And so return to you, and nothing else?

[63]*secrets*

15 PORTIA: Yes, bring me word, boy, if thy lord look well,
     For he went sickly forth; and take good note
     What Caesar doth, what suitors press to him.
     Hark, boy, what noise is that?
LUCIUS: I hear none, madam.
20 PORTIA: Prithee, listen well.
     I heard a bustling rumor like a fray,[64]
     And the wind brings it from the Capitol.
LUCIUS: Sooth, madam, I hear nothing.

Enter the Soothsayer.

PORTIA: Come hither, fellow; which way hast thou been?
25 SOOTHSAYER: At mine own house, good lady.
PORTIA: What is't o'clock?
SOOTHSAYER: About the ninth hour, lady.
PORTIA: Is Caesar yet gone to the Capitol?
SOOTHSAYER: Madam, not yet. I go to take my stand
30   To see him pass on to the Capitol.
PORTIA: Thou hast some suit[65] to Caesar, hast thou not?
SOOTHSAYER: That I have, lady. If it will please Caesar
     To be so good to Caesar as to hear me,
     I shall beseech him to befriend himself.
35 PORTIA: Why, know'st thou any harm's intended towards him?
SOOTHSAYER: None that I know will be, much that I fear may
            chance.
     Good morrow to you. Here the street is narrow,
     The throng that follows Caesar at the heels,
     Of senators, of praetors, common suitors,
40   Will crowd a feeble man almost to death.
     I'll get me to a place more void[66] and there
     Speak to great Caesar as he comes along.   *Exit.*
PORTIA: I must go in. Ay me, how weak a thing
     The heart of woman is! O Brutus,
45   The heavens speed thee in thine enterprise!
     Sure, the boy heard me. Brutus hath a suit
     That Caesar will not grant. O, I grow faint.
     Run, Lucius, and commend me to my lord;
     Say I am merry. Come to me again,
50   And bring me word what he doth say to thee.
                     Exeunt [severally.]

[64] *confused noise, as in a fight*

[65] *matter to present*

[66] *less crowded*

ACT III

The conspirators kill caesar.
Antony says he will join
the conspirators but
vows in secret to avenge
caesar.

[SCENE I
Rome. The Capitol]

[Flourish. Enter Caesar, Brutus, Cassius, Casca, Decius, Metellus [Cimber], Trebonius, Cinna, Antony, Lepidus, Artimedorus, Publius, [Popilius]; and the Soothsayer.]

CAESAR: The ides of March are come.

SOOTHSAYER: Ay, Caesar, but not gone.

ARTEMIDORUS: Hail, Caesar! Read this schedule.[1]   [1]document

DECIUS: Trebonius doth desire you to o'er read,[2]   [2]read over

5   At your best leisure, this his humble suit.

ARTEMIDORUS: O Caesar, read mine first, for mine's a suit

    That touches Caesar nearer. Read it, great Caesar.

CAESAR: What touches us ourself shall be last served.
believes public self is invulnerable, so strong personal self cannot be harmed

ARTEMIDORUS: Delay not, Caesar; read it instantly.

10 CAESAR: What, is the fellow mad?
doesn't think anyone could not love him to conspire against him

PUBLIUS: Sirrah, give place.

CASSIUS: What, urge you your petitions in the street?

    Come to the Capitol.

POPILIUS: I wish your enterprise today may thrive.

15 CASSIUS: What enterprise, Popilius?

POPILIUS: Fare you well.

BRUTUS: What said Popilius Lena?

CASSIUS: He wish'd today our enterprise might thrive.

    I fear our purpose is discovered.

20 BRUTUS: Look, how he makes to Caesar. Mark him.

CASSIUS: Casca,

    Be sudden, for we fear prevention.

    Brutus, what shall be done? If this be known,

    Cassius or Caesar never shall turn back,

25   For I will slay myself.

BRUTUS: Cassius, be constant.

Popilius Lena speaks not of our purposes;

For, look, he smiles, and Caesar doth not change.

CASSIUS: Trebonius knows his time, for, look you, Brutus,

30   He draws Mark Antony out of the way.

                      [Exeunt Antony and Trebonius.]

DECIUS: Where is Metellus Cimber? Let him go,

And presently³ prefer⁴ his suit to Caesar.

BRUTUS: He is address'd; press near and second him.

CINNA: Casca, you are the first that rears your hand.

35   CAESAR: Are we all ready? What is now amiss

That Caesar and his Senate must redress?

METELLUS: Most high, most mighty, and most puissant⁵ Caesar,

Metellus Cimber throws before thy seat

An humble heart.

40   CAESAR: I must prevent thee, Cimber.

These couchings⁶ and these lowly courtesies

Might fire the blood of ordinary men

And turn preordinance⁷ and first decree

Into the law of children.⁸ Be not fond

45   To think that Caesar bears such rebel blood

That will be thaw'd from the true quality

With that which melteth fools, I mean sweet words,

Low-crooked court'sies, and base spaniel-fawning.

Thy brother by decree is banished.

50   If thou dost bend and pray and fawn for him,

I spurn thee like a cur out of my way.

Know, Caesar doth not wrong, nor without cause

Will he be satisfied.

METELLUS: Is there no voice more worthy than my own,

55   To sound more sweetly in great Caesar's ear

For the repealing of my banish'd brother?

BRUTUS: I kiss thy hand, but not in flattery, Caesar,

Desiring thee that Publius Cimber may

Have an immediate freedom of repeal.

60   CAESAR: What, Brutus?

CASSIUS: Pardon, Caesar! Caesar, pardon!

As low as to thy foot doth Cassius fall

To beg enfranchisement for Publius Cimber.

CAESAR: I could be well moved,⁹ if I were as you;

Margin glosses:

³*immediately*

⁴*bring forth*

⁵*powerful*

⁶*bowing and scraping*

⁷*Caesar's initial decision*

⁸*rules in a children's game*

⁹*my mind could be changed*

Handwritten note: brother of Metellus has been banished for being a conspirator

65   If I could pray to move, prayers would move me;

       But I am constant as the northern star,

       Of whose true-fix'd and resting quality

       There is no fellow[10] in the firmament.

       The skies are painted with unnumber'd sparks;

70   They are all fire and every one doth shine;

       But there's but one in all doth hold his place.

       So in the world, 'tis furnish'd well with men,

       And men are flesh and blood, and apprehensive;[11]

       Yet in the number I do know but one

75   That unassailable holds on his rank,

       Unshaked of motion; and that I am he,

       Let me a little show it, even in this;

       That I was constant Cimber should be banish'd,

       And constant do remain to keep him so.

80   CINNA: O Caesar,—

       CAESAR: Hence! Wilt thou lift up Olympus?[12]

       DECIUS: Great Caesar—

       CAESAR: Doth not Brutus bootless kneel?

       CASCA: Speak, hands, for me!

They stab Caesar.

85   CAESAR: Et tu, Brute?[13] Then fall, Caesar!   *Dies.*

       CINNA: Liberty! Freedom! Tyranny is dead!

         Run hence, proclaim, cry it about the streets.

       CASSIUS: Some to the common pulpits and cry out

         "Liberty, freedom, and enfranchisement!"

90   BRUTUS: People, and senators, be not affrighted,

         Fly not, stand still; ambition's debt is paid.

       CASCA: Go to the pulpit, Brutus.

       DECIUS: And Cassius too.

       BRUTUS: Where's Publius?

95   CINNA: Here, quite confounded with this mutiny.

       METELLUS: Stand fast together, lest some friend of Caesar's

         Should chance—

       BRUTUS: Talk not of standing. Publius, good cheer,

         There is no harm intended to your person,

100   Nor to no Roman else. So tell them, Publius.

       CASSIUS: And leave us, Publius, lest that the people

---

[10] equal

[11] able to reason and understand

[12] in classical mythology, the mountain where the gods lived

[13] Even you, Brutus?

Rushing on us should do your age some mischief.

BRUTUS: Do so, and let no man abide[14] this deed

But we the doers.

[Re-]enter Trebonius.]

105 CASSIUS: Where is Antony?

TREBONIUS: Fled to his house amazed.

Men, wives, and children stare, cry out, and run

As it were doomsday.

BRUTUS: Fates, we will know your pleasures.

110 That we shall die, we know; 'tis but the time

And drawing days out that men stand upon.[15]

CASSIUS: Why, he that cuts off twenty years of life

Cuts off so many years of fearing death.

BRUTUS: Grant that, and then is death a benefit;

115 So are we Caesar's friends that have abridged

His time of fearing death. Stoop, Romans, stoop,

And let us bathe our hands in Caesar's blood

Up to the elbows, and besmear our swords;

Then walk we forth, even to the market-place,

120 And waving our red weapons o'er our heads,

Let's all cry, "Peace, freedom, and liberty!"

CASSIUS: Stoop then, and wash. How many ages hence

Shall this our lofty scene be acted over

In states unborn and accents yet unknown!

125 BRUTUS: How many times shall Caesar bleed in sport,

That now on Pompey's basis[16] lies along

No worthier than the dust!

CASSIUS: So oft as that shall be,

So often shall the knot[17] of us be call'd

130 The men that gave their country liberty.

DECIUS: What, shall we forth?

CASSIUS: Ay, every man away.

Brutus shall lead, and we will grace his heels

With the most boldest and best hearts of Rome.

Enter a Servant.

135 BRUTUS: Soft, who comes here? A friend of Antony's.

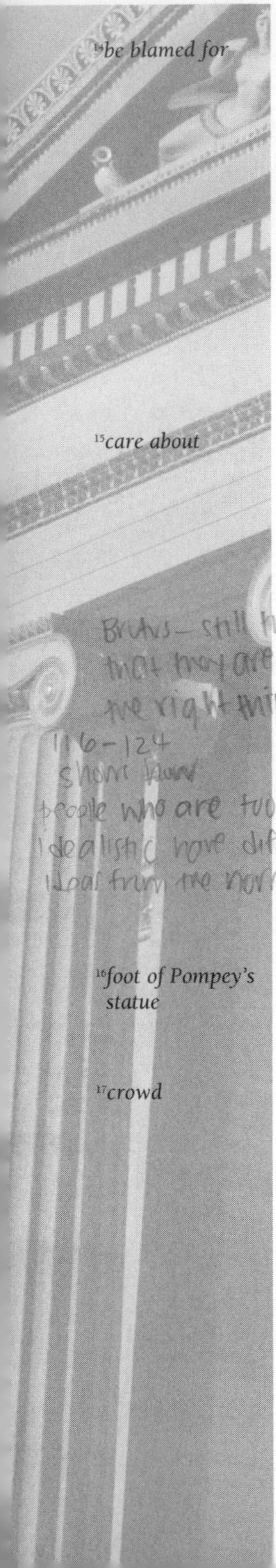

[14]*be blamed for*

[15]*care about*

[16]*foot of Pompey's statue*

[17]*crowd*

[handwritten margin notes:]
Brutus — still thinking that they are doing the right thing

116–124 show how people who are too idealistic have different ideal from the normal

idealistic

Brutus expects people to cheer for him; thinks Romans will cheer for what they've done

SERVANT: Thus, Brutus, did my master bid me kneel,
 Thus did Mark Antony bid me fall down,
 And, being prostrate, thus he bade me say:
 Brutus is noble, wise, valiant, and honest;
140 Caesar was mighty, bold, royal, and loving.
 Say I love Brutus and I honor him;
 Say I fear'd Caesar, honor'd him, and loved him.
 If Brutus will vouchsafe that Antony
 May safely come to him and be resolved[18]

[18]*learn to his satisfaction*

145 How Caesar hath deserved to lie in death,
 Mark Antony shall not love Caesar dead
 So well as Brutus living, but will follow
 The fortunes and affairs of noble Brutus
 Thorough the hazards of this untrod[19] state

[19]*new*

150 With all true faith. So says my master Antony.
BRUTUS: Thy master is a wise and valiant Roman;
 I never thought him worse.
 Tell him, so please him come unto this place,
 He shall be satisfied and, by my honor,
155 Depart untouch'd.
SERVANT: I'll fetch him presently.   *Exit servant.*
BRUTUS: I know that we shall have him well to friend.
CASSIUS: I wish we may, but yet have I a mind
 That fears him much, and my misgiving still
160 Falls shrewdly to the purpose.[20]

[20]*my negative feelings are usually right*

[Re-]enter Antony.]

BRUTUS: But here comes Antony. Welcome, Mark Antony.
ANTONY: O mighty Caesar! Dost thou lie so low?
 Are all thy conquests, glories, triumphs, spoils,
 Shrunk to this little measure? Fare thee well.
165 I know not, gentlemen, what you intend,
 Who else must be let blood, who else is rank.[21]

[21]*"foul," but also "having too much power"*

 If I myself, there is no hour so fit
 As Caesar's death's hour, nor no instrument
 Of half that worth as those your swords, made rich
170 With the most noble blood of all this world.
 I do beseech ye, if you bear me hard,
 Now, whilst your purpled hands do reek and smoke,

[handwritten margin note: asking the conspirators to kill him so they can try to get him on their side.]

Fulfill your pleasure. Live a thousand years,
I shall not find myself so apt to die;
175   No place will please me so, no mean of death,
As here by Caesar, and by you cut off,
The choice and master spirits of this age.
BRUTUS: O Antony, beg not your death of us!
Though now we must appear bloody and cruel,
180   As, by our hands and this our present act,
You see we do, yet see you but our hands
And this the bleeding business they have done.
Our hearts you see not; they are pitiful;
And pity to the general wrong of Rome—
185   As fire drives out fire, so pity pity—
Hath done this deed on Caesar. For your part,
To you our swords have leaden points, Mark Antony;
Our arms in strength of malice, and our hearts
Of brothers' temper,[22] do receive you in
190   With all kind love, good thoughts, and reverence.
CASSIUS: Your voice shall be as strong as any man's
In the disposing of new dignities.[23]
BRUTUS: Only be patient till we have appeased
The multitude, beside themselves with fear,
195   And then we will deliver you the cause[24]
Why I, that did love Caesar when I struck him,
Have thus proceeded.
ANTONY: I doubt not of your wisdom.
Let each man render me his bloody hand.
200   First, Marcus Brutus, will I shake with you;
Next, Caius Cassius, do I take your hand;
Now, Decius Brutus, yours; now yours, Metellus;
Yours, Cinna; and, my valiant Casca, yours;
Though last, not least in love, yours, good Trebonius.
205   Gentlemen all,—alas, what shall I say?
My credit now stands on such slippery ground,
That one of two bad ways you must conceit me,
Either a coward or a flatterer.
That I did love thee, Caesar, O, 'tis true!
210   If then thy spirit look upon us now,
Shall it not grieve thee dearer than thy death
To see thy Antony making his peace,

[22] our bloodstained arms and our virtuous hearts

[23] handing out political offices

[24] explain

• in shaking hands —
is a conspirator
but is a conspirator
against Brutus & Cassius,
vengeance for Caesar

shaking
hands w/
each of
conspirators

Shaking the bloody fingers of thy foes,
Most noble! In the presence of thy corse?[25]

215 Had I as many eyes as thou hast wounds,
Weeping as fast as they stream forth thy blood,
It would become me better than to close
In terms of friendship with thine enemies.
Pardon me, Julius! Here wast thou bay'd,[26] brave hart,[27]

220 Here didst thou fall, and here thy hunters stand,
Sign'd in thy spoil, and crimson'd in thy lethe.[28]
O world, thou wast the forest to this hart,
And this, indeed, O world, the heart of thee.
How like a deer strucken by many princes

225 Dost thou here lie!

CASSIUS: Mark Antony,—

ANTONY: Pardon me, Caius Cassius.
The enemies of Caesar shall say this:
Then, in a friend, it is cold modesty.[29]

230 CASSIUS: I blame you not for praising Caesar so;
But what compact[30] mean you to have with us?
Will you be prick'd[31] in number of our friends,
Or shall we on, and not depend on you?

ANTONY: Therefore I took your hands, but was indeed

235 Sway'd from the point by looking down on Caesar.
Friends am I with you all and love you all,
Upon this hope that you shall give me reasons
Why and wherein Caesar was dangerous.

BRUTUS: Or else were this a savage spectacle.

240 Our reasons are so full of good regard
That were you, Antony, the son of Caesar,
You should be satisfied.

ANTONY: That's all I seek;
And am moreover suitor that I may

245 Produce his body to the marketplace,
And in the pulpit, as becomes a friend,
Speak in the order of his funeral.

BRUTUS: You shall, Mark Antony.

CASSIUS: Brutus, a word with you.

250 *[Aside to Brutus.]* You know not what you do. Do not consent
That Antony speak in his funeral.
Know you how much the people may be moved

[25]*corpse*

[26]*cornered*

[27]*a common Elizabethan pun, meaning both "deer" and "heart"*

[28]*blood of the deer*

[29]*hardly overstatement*

[30]*agreement*

[31]*added to the list (written with a quill pen)*

By that which he will utter?

BRUTUS: By your pardon,

255 I will myself into the pulpit first,

And show the reason of our Caesar's death.

What Antony shall speak, I will protest

He speaks by leave and by permission,

And that we are contented Caesar shall

260 Have all true rites and lawful ceremonies.

It shall advantage[32] more than do us wrong.

CASSIUS: I know not what may fall; I like it not.

BRUTUS: Mark Antony, here, take you Caesar's body.

You shall not in your funeral speech blame us,

265 But speak all good you can devise of Caesar,

And say you do't by our permission,

Else shall you not have any hand at all

About his funeral. And you shall speak

In the same pulpit whereto I am going,

270 After my speech is ended.

ANTONY: Be it so,

I do desire no more.

BRUTUS: Prepare the body then, and follow us.

Exeunt [all but] Antony.

ANTONY: O, pardon me, thou bleeding piece of earth,

275 That I am meek and gentle with these butchers!

Thou art the ruins of the noblest man

That ever lived in the tide of times.

Woe to the hand that shed this costly blood!

Over thy wounds now do I prophesy

280 Which like dumb mouths do ope their ruby lips

To beg the voice and utterance of my tongue,

A curse shall light upon the limbs of men;

Domestic fury and fierce civil strife

Shall cumber[33] all the parts of Italy;

285 Blood and destruction shall be so in use,

And dreadful objects so familiar,

That mothers shall but smile when they behold

Their infants quarter'd[34] with the hands of war;

All pity choked with custom of fell deeds,

290 And Caesar's spirit ranging[35] for revenge,

With Ate[36] by his side come hot from hell,

[32]do us good

[33]weigh heavy on

[34]cut into four pieces

[35]wandering

[36]goddess of vengeance

    Shall in these confines with a monarch's voice

    Cry "Havoc!" and let slip the dogs of war,

    That this foul deed shall smell above the earth

295   With carrion men, groaning for burial.

Enter Octavius' Servant.   Caesar's adopted son

    You serve Octavius Caesar, do you not?

SERVANT: I do, Mark Antony.

ANTONY: Caesar did write for him to come to Rome.

SERVANT: He did receive his letters, and is coming,

300   And bid me say to you by word of mouth—

    O Caesar!

ANTONY: Thy heart is big; get thee apart and weep.

    Passion, I see, is catching, for mine eyes,

    Seeing those beads of sorrow stand in thine,

305   Began to water. Is thy master coming?

SERVANT: He lies tonight within seven leagues[37] of Rome.   [37]*21 miles*

ANTONY: Post back with speed and tell him what hath chanced.

    Here is a mourning Rome, a dangerous Rome,

    No Rome of safety for Octavius yet;

310   Hie hence, and tell him so. Yet stay awhile,

    Thou shalt not back till I have borne this corse

    Into the market-place. There shall I try,

    In my oration, how the people take

    The cruel issue[38] of these bloody men,   [38]*result*

315   According to the which thou shalt discourse

    To young Octavius of the state of things.

    Lend me your hand.

                             Exeunt.

[handwritten: crowd]
[handwritten: calm →angry]

[SCENE II
The Forum.]

[handwritten: Brutus, then Antony makes speeches, manipulating the crowd]

Enter Brutus and goes into the pulpit, and Cassius, with the Plebeians.[39]

[39]*The Plebeians were the common people of Rome; the rabble*

CITIZENS: We will be satisfied! Let us be satisfied!
BRUTUS: Then follow me and give me audience, friends.
    Cassius, go you into the other street
5   And part the numbers.[40]

[40]*crowd*

    Those that will hear me speak, let 'em stay here;
    Those that will follow Cassius, go with him;
    And public reasons shall be rendered
    Of Caesar's death.
10 FIRST CITIZEN: I will hear Brutus speak.
SECOND CITIZEN: I will hear Cassius and compare their reasons,
    When severally[41] we hear them rendered.

[41]*one by one*

                  [Exit Cassius, with some of the Citizens.]
THIRD CITIZEN: The noble Brutus is ascended. Silence!
BRUTUS: Be patient till the last.
15   Romans, countrymen, and lovers! Hear me for my cause, and be silent, that you may hear. Believe me for mine honor, and have respect to mine honor, that you may believe. Censure me in your wisdom, and awake your senses, that you may the better judge. If there be any in
20   this assembly, any dear friend of Caesar's, to him I say that Brutus' love to Caesar was no less than his. If then that friend demand why Brutus rose against Caesar, this is my answer: Not that I loved Caesar less, but that I loved Rome more. Had you rather Caesar were living and die all slaves,
25   than that Caesar were dead to live all freemen? As Caesar loved me, I weep for him; as he was fortunate, I rejoice at it; as he was valiant, I honor him; but as he was ambitious, I slew him. There is tears for his love, joy for his fortune, honor for his valor, and death for his ambition. Who is
30   here so base that would be a bondman? If any, speak, for him have I offended. Who is here so rude that would not be a Roman? If any, speak, for him have I offended. Who is here so vile that will not love his country? If any, speak, for him have I offended. I pause for a reply.

35 ALL: None, Brutus, none.

BRUTUS: Then none have I offended. I have done no more to
Caesar than you shall do to Brutus. The question of his death
is enrolled in the Capitol, his glory not extenuated,[42] wherein
he was worthy, nor his offenses enforced, for which he suf-
40 fered death.

lessened [42]

Enter Antony [and others] with Caesar's body.

Here comes his body, mourned by Mark Antony, who,
though he had no hand in his death, shall receive the benefit
45 of his dying, a place in the commonwealth, as which of you
shall not? With this I depart—that, as I slew my best lover
for the good of Rome, I have the same dagger for myself,
when it shall please my country to need my death.

ALL : Live, Brutus, live, live!

50 FIRST CITIZEN: Bring him with triumph home unto his house.

SECOND CITIZEN: Give him a statue with his ancestors.

THIRD CITIZEN: Let him be Caesar.

FOURTH CITIZEN: Caesar's better parts
Shall be crown'd in Brutus.

55 FIRST CITIZEN: We'll bring him to his house with shouts and
clamors.

BRUTUS: My countrymen—

SECOND CITIZEN: Peace! Silence! Brutus speaks.

FIRST CITIZEN: Peace, ho!

60 BRUTUS: Good countrymen, let me depart alone,
And, for my sake, stay here with Antony.
Do grace to Caesar's corse, and grace his speech
Tending to Caesar's glories, which Mark Antony,
By our permission, is allow'd to make.
65 I do entreat you, not a man depart,
Save I alone, till Antony have spoke.   *Exit.*

FIRST CITIZEN: Stay, ho, and let us hear Mark Antony.

THIRD CITIZEN: Let him go up into the public chair;
We'll hear him. Noble Antony, go up.

70 ANTONY: For Brutus' sake, I am beholding[43] to you.

FOURTH CITIZEN: What does he say of Brutus?

THIRD CITIZEN: He says, for Brutus' sake,
He finds himself beholding to us all.

FOURTH CITIZEN: 'Twere best he speak no harm of Brutus here.

obliged [43]

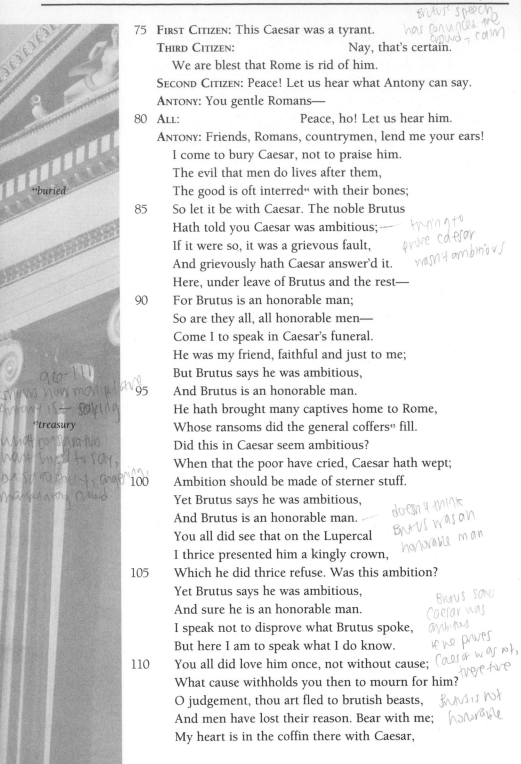

75 FIRST CITIZEN: This Caesar was a tyrant.

THIRD CITIZEN: Nay, that's certain.

   We are blest that Rome is rid of him.

SECOND CITIZEN: Peace! Let us hear what Antony can say.

ANTONY: You gentle Romans—

80 ALL: Peace, ho! Let us hear him.

ANTONY: Friends, Romans, countrymen, lend me your ears!

   I come to bury Caesar, not to praise him.

   The evil that men do lives after them,

   The good is oft interred[44] with their bones;

85   So let it be with Caesar. The noble Brutus

   Hath told you Caesar was ambitious;

   If it were so, it was a grievous fault,

   And grievously hath Caesar answer'd it.

   Here, under leave of Brutus and the rest—

90   For Brutus is an honorable man;

   So are they all, all honorable men—

   Come I to speak in Caesar's funeral.

   He was my friend, faithful and just to me;

   But Brutus says he was ambitious,

95   And Brutus is an honorable man.

   He hath brought many captives home to Rome,

   Whose ransoms did the general coffers[45] fill.

   Did this in Caesar seem ambitious?

   When that the poor have cried, Caesar hath wept;

100 Ambition should be made of sterner stuff.

   Yet Brutus says he was ambitious,

   And Brutus is an honorable man.

   You all did see that on the Lupercal

   I thrice presented him a kingly crown,

105 Which he did thrice refuse. Was this ambition?

   Yet Brutus says he was ambitious,

   And sure he is an honorable man.

   I speak not to disprove what Brutus spoke,

   But here I am to speak what I do know.

110 You all did love him once, not without cause;

   What cause withholds you then to mourn for him?

   O judgement, thou art fled to brutish beasts,

   And men have lost their reason. Bear with me;

   My heart is in the coffin there with Caesar,

[44] *buried*

[45] *treasury*

115   And I must pause till it come back to me.
       FIRST CITIZEN: Methinks there is much reason in his sayings.
       SECOND CITIZEN: If thou consider rightly of the matter,
           Caesar has had great wrong.
       THIRD CITIZEN: Has he, masters?
120   I fear there will a worse come in his place.
       FOURTH CITIZEN: Mark'd ye his words? He would not take the
                   crown;
           Therefore 'tis certain he was not ambitious.
       FIRST CITIZEN: If it be found so, some will dear abide it.
125   SECOND CITIZEN: Poor soul, his eyes are red as fire with weeping.
       THIRD CITIZEN: There's not a nobler man in Rome than Antony.
       FOURTH CITIZEN: Now mark him, he begins again to speak.
       ANTONY: But yesterday the word of Caesar might
           Have stood against the world. Now lies he there,
130   And none so poor to do him reverence.[46]
           O masters! If I were disposed to stir
           Your hearts and minds to mutiny and rage,
           I should do Brutus wrong and Cassius wrong,
           Who, you all know, are honorable men.
135   I will not do them wrong; I rather choose
           To wrong the dead, to wrong myself and you,
           Than I will wrong such honorable men.
           But here's a parchment with the seal of Caesar;
           I found it in his closet, 'tis his will.
140   Let but the commons hear this testament—
           Which, pardon me, I do not mean to read—
           And they would go and kiss dead Caesar's wounds
           And dip their napkins in his sacred blood,
           Yea, beg a hair of him for memory,
145   And, dying, mention it within their wills,
           Bequeathing it as a rich legacy
           Unto their issue.[47]
       FOURTH CITIZEN: We'll hear the will. Read it, Mark Antony.
       ALL: The will, the will! We will hear Caesar's will.
150   ANTONY: Have patience, gentle friends, I must not read it;
           It is not meet you know how Caesar loved you.
           You are not wood, you are not stones, but men;
           And, being men, hearing the will of Caesar,
           It will inflame you, it will make you mad.

[46]*no one will stoop to the level of honoring him*

[47]*heirs*

155   'Tis good you know not that you are his heirs,
For if you should, O, what would come of it!
FOURTH CITIZEN: Read the will; we'll hear it, Antony.
You shall read us the will, Caesar's will.
ANTONY: Will you be patient? Will you stay a while?
160   I have o'ershot myself[48] to tell you of it.
I fear I wrong the honorable men
Whose daggers have stabb'd Caesar; I do fear it.
FOURTH CITIZEN: They were traitors. "Honorable men!"
ALL: The will! The testament!
165 SECOND CITIZEN: They were villains, murderers. The will!
Read the will!
ANTONY: You will compel me then to read the will?
Then make a ring about the corse of Caesar,
And let me show you him that made the will.
170   Shall I descend? And will you give me leave?
ALL: Come down.
SECOND CITIZEN: Descend.
THIRD CITIZEN: You shall have leave.
FOURTH CITIZEN: A ring, stand round.
175 FIRST CITIZEN: Stand from the hearse, stand from the body.
SECOND CITIZEN: Room for Antony, most noble Antony.
ANTONY: Nay, press not so upon me, stand far off.
ALL: Stand back; room, bear back!
ANTONY: If you have tears, prepare to shed them now.
180   You all do know this mantle.[49] I remember
The first time ever Caesar put it on;
'Twas on a summer's evening, in his tent,
That day he overcame the Nervii.[50]
Look, in this place ran Cassius' dagger through;
185   See what a rent the envious Casca made;
Through this the well-beloved Brutus stabb'd;
And as he pluck'd his cursed steel away,
Mark how the blood of Caesar follow'd it,
As rushing out of doors, to be resolved[51]
190   If Brutus so unkindly knock'd, or no;
For Brutus, as you know, was Caesar's angel.
Judge, O you gods, how dearly Caesar loved him!
This was the most unkindest cut of all;
For when the noble Caesar saw him stab,

[48]acted without proper judgment
[49]cloak
[50]tribe defeated by Caesar in 57 B.C.
[51]certain

195   Ingratitude, more strong than traitors' arms,
        Quite vanquish'd him. Then burst his mighty heart,
        And, in his mantle muffling up his face,
        Even at the base of Pompey's statue,
        Which all the while ran blood, great Caesar fell.
200   O, what a fall was there, my countrymen!
        Then I, and you, and all of us fell down,
        Whilst bloody treason flourish'd over us.
        O, now you weep, and I perceive you feel
        The dint[52] of pity. These are gracious drops.
205   Kind souls, what weep you when you but behold
        Our Caesar's vesture wounded? Look you here,
        Here is himself, marr'd, as you see, with traitors.
    FIRST CITIZEN: O piteous spectacle!
    SECOND CITIZEN: O noble Caesar!
210 THIRD CITIZEN: O woeful day!
    FOURTH CITIZEN: O traitors, villains!
    FIRST CITIZEN: O most bloody sight!
    SECOND CITIZEN: We will be revenged.
    ALL: Revenge! About! Seek! Burn! Fire! Kill!
215   Slay! Let not a traitor live!
    ANTONY: Stay, countrymen.
    FIRST CITIZEN: Peace there! Hear the noble Antony.
    SECOND CITIZEN: We'll hear him, we'll follow him, we'll die with
        him.
220 ANTONY: Good friends, sweet friends, let me not stir you up
        To such a sudden flood of mutiny.
        They that have done this deed are honorable.
        What private griefs they have, alas, I know not,
        That made them do it. They are wise and honorable,
225   And will, no doubt, with reasons answer you.
        I come not, friends, to steal away your hearts.
        I am no orator, as Brutus is;
        But, as you know me all, a plain blunt man,
        That love my friend, and that they know full well
230   That gave me public leave to speak of him.
        For I have neither wit, nor words, nor worth,
        Action, nor utterance, nor the power of speech,
        To stir men's blood. I only speak right on;
        I tell you that which you yourselves do know;

[52]*effect*

235 Show you sweet Caesar's wounds, poor poor dumb mouths,
And bid them speak for me. But were I Brutus,
And Brutus Antony, there were an Antony
Would ruffle up your spirits and put a tongue
In every wound of Caesar that should move
240 The stones of Rome to rise and mutiny.
ALL: We'll mutiny.
FIRST CITIZEN: We'll burn the house of Brutus.
THIRD CITIZEN: Away, then! Come, seek the conspirators.
ANTONY: Yet hear me, countrymen; yet hear me speak.
245 ALL: Peace, ho! Hear Antony, most noble Antony!
ANTONY: Why, friends, you go to do you know not what.
Wherein hath Caesar thus deserved your loves?
Alas, you know not; I must tell you then.
You have forgot the will I told you of.
250 ALL: Most true, the will! Let's stay and hear the will.
ANTONY: Here is the will, and under Caesar's seal.
To every Roman citizen he gives,
To every several[53] man, seventy-five drachmas.
SECOND CITIZEN: Most noble Caesar! We'll revenge his death.
255 THIRD CITIZEN: O royal Caesar!
ANTONY: Hear me with patience.
ALL: Peace, ho!
ANTONY: Moreover, he hath left you all his walks,
His private arbors, and new-planted orchards,
260 On this side Tiber; he hath left them you,
And to your heirs for ever; common pleasures,
To walk abroad and recreate yourselves.
Here was a Caesar! When comes such another?
FIRST CITIZEN: Never, never. Come, away, away!
265 We'll burn his body in the holy place
And with the brands fire the traitors' houses.
Take up the body.
SECOND CITIZEN: Go fetch fire.
THIRD CITIZEN: Pluck down benches.
270 FOURTH CITIZEN: Pluck down forms, windows, any thing.

Exit Plebeians [with the body.]

ANTONY: Now let it work. Mischief, thou art afoot,[54]
Take thou what course thou wilt.

[53]*individual*

[54]*on the loose*

[Enter a Servant.]

    How now, fellow?

SERVANT: Sir, Octavius is already come to Rome.

275 ANTONY: Where is he?

SERVANT: He and Lepidus are at Caesar's house.

ANTONY: And thither will I straight[55] to visit him.

    He comes upon a wish. Fortune is merry,

    And in this mood will give us any thing.

280 SERVANT: I heard him say, Brutus and Cassius

    Are rid like madmen through the gates of Rome.

ANTONY: Belike they had some notice of the people,

    How I had moved them. Bring me to Octavius.

                              Exeunt.

[55]*immediately*

[SCENE III
A street.]

the crowd kills a random poet because his name is Cinna, the same as one of the conspirators

Enter Cinna the poet, and after him the Plebeians.

CINNA: I dreamt tonight that I did feast with Caesar,

    And things unluckily charge my fantasy.[56]

    I have no will to wander forth of doors,

    Yet something leads me forth.

5 FIRST CITIZEN: What is your name?

SECOND CITIZEN: Whither are you going?

THIRD CITIZEN: Where do you dwell?

FOURTH CITIZEN: Are you a married man or a bachelor?

SECOND CITIZEN: Answer every man directly.

10 FIRST CITIZEN: Ay, and briefly.

FOURTH CITIZEN: Ay, and wisely.

THIRD CITIZEN: Ay, and truly, you were best.

CINNA: What is my name? Whither am I going? Where do I

    dwell? Am I a married man or a bachelor? Then, to answer

15   every man directly and briefly, wisely and truly: wisely I say,

    I am a bachelor.

SECOND CITIZEN: That's as much as to say, they are fools that

    marry. You'll bear me a bang for that, I fear. Proceed directly.

CINNA: Directly, I am going to Caesar's funeral.

[56]*make my dream seem negative*

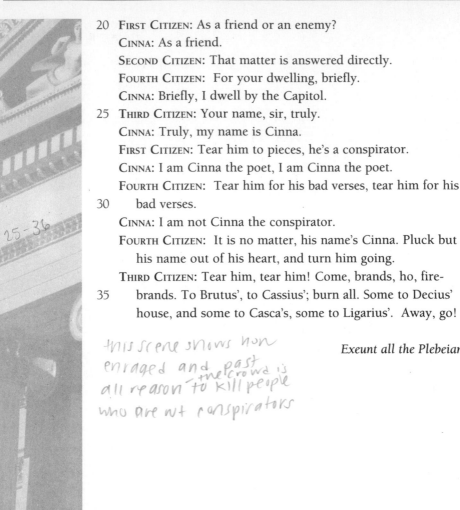

20 FIRST CITIZEN: As a friend or an enemy?

CINNA: As a friend.

SECOND CITIZEN: That matter is answered directly.

FOURTH CITIZEN: For your dwelling, briefly.

CINNA: Briefly, I dwell by the Capitol.

25 THIRD CITIZEN: Your name, sir, truly.

CINNA: Truly, my name is Cinna.

FIRST CITIZEN: Tear him to pieces, he's a conspirator.

CINNA: I am Cinna the poet, I am Cinna the poet.

FOURTH CITIZEN: Tear him for his bad verses, tear him for his

30   bad verses.

CINNA: I am not Cinna the conspirator.

FOURTH CITIZEN: It is no matter, his name's Cinna. Pluck but
his name out of his heart, and turn him going.

THIRD CITIZEN: Tear him, tear him! Come, brands, ho, fire-

35   brands. To Brutus', to Cassius'; burn all. Some to Decius'
house, and some to Casca's, some to Ligarius'. Away, go!

Exeunt all the Plebeians.

25-36

this scene shows how
enraged and past
the crowd is
all reason to kill people
who are not conspirators

JULIUS CAESAR

ACT IV

[SCENE I
A house in Rome.]

Enter Antony, Octavius, and Lepidus.

ANTONY: These many then shall die, their names are prick'd.
OCTAVIUS: Your brother too must die; consent you, Lepidus?
LEPIDUS: I do consent—
OCTAVIUS: Prick him down, Antony.
5 LEPIDUS: Upon condition Publius shall not live,
      Who is your sister's son, Mark Antony.
ANTONY: He shall not live; look, with a spot I damn him.
      But, Lepidus, go you to Caesar's house,
      Fetch the will hither, and we shall determine
10   How to cut off some charge in legacies.
   LEPIDUS: What, shall I find you here?
   OCTAVIUS: Or here, or at the Capitol.   *Exit Lepidus.*
   ANTONY: This is a slight unmeritable man,
      Meet to be sent on errands. Is it fit,
15   The three-fold world divided, he should stand
      One of the three to share it?
   OCTAVIUS: So you thought him,
      And took his voice who should be prick'd to die
      In our black sentence and proscription.[1]
20 ANTONY: Octavius, I have seen more days than you,
      And though we lay these honors on this man
      To ease ourselves of divers slanderous[2] loads,
      He shall but bear them as the ass bears gold,
      To groan and sweat under the business,
25   Either led or driven, as we point the way;
      And having brought our treasure where we will,
      Then take we down his load and turn him off,

[1]*condemnation*

[2]*many insulting*

63

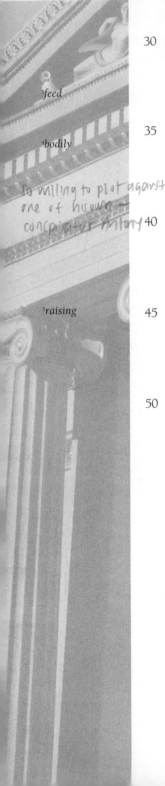

Like to the empty ass, to shake his ears
And graze in commons.

30 OCTAVIUS: You may do your will,
But he's a tried and valiant soldier.

ANTONY: So is my horse, Octavius, and for that
I do appoint him store of provender.³

feed

It is a creature that I teach to fight,

35   To wind, to stop, to run directly on,
His corporal⁴ motion govern'd by my spirit.

bodily

And, in some taste, is Lepidus but so:
He must be taught, and train'd, and bid go forth;
A barren-spirited fellow, one that feeds

40   On objects, arts, and imitations,
Which, out of use and staled by other men,
Begin his fashion. Do not talk of him
But as a property. And now, Octavius,
Listen great things. Brutus and Cassius

raising

45   Are levying⁵ powers; we must straight make head;
Therefore let our alliance be combined,
Our best friends made, our means stretch'd;
And let us presently go sit in council,
How covert matters may be best disclosed,

50   And open perils surest answered.

OCTAVIUS: Let us do so, for we are at the stake,
And bay'd about with many enemies;
And some that smile have in their hearts, I fear,
Millions of mischiefs.   *Exeunt.*

[SCENE II
Camp near Sardis.
Before Brutus' tent.]

*Drum Enter Brutus, Lucilius, [Lucius] and the Army; Titinius and
Pindarus meet them.*

BRUTUS: Stand, ho!
LUCILIUS: Give the word, ho, and stand.
BRUTUS: What now, Lucilius, is Cassius near?

Handwritten margin notes:
- Octavius do what you want but he is a good soldier
- Antony - 'he's stupid, let's ditch him'
- explains Lepidus as an instrument - just to use for their own purposes
- So willing to plot against one of his own — conspirator Antony
- Disagreement between Brutus & Cassius

LUCILIUS: He is at hand, and Pindarus is come
5   To do you salutation⁶ from his master.

                         ⁶greet you

BRUTUS: He greets me well. Your master, Pindarus,
In his own change,⁷ or by ill officers,⁷
Hath given me some worthy cause to wish
Things done undone; but if he be at hand,
10   I shall be satisfied.

                         ⁷either through his own intention or through others' representation of him

PINDARUS: I do not doubt
But that my noble master will appear
Such as he is, full of regard and honor.
BRUTUS: He is not doubted. A word, Lucilius,
15   How he received you. Let me be resolved.
LUCILIUS: With courtesy and with respect enough,
But not with such familiar instances,⁸

                         ⁸gestures

Nor with such free and friendly conference,
As he hath used of old.
20 BRUTUS: Thou hast described
A hot friend cooling. Ever note, Lucilius,
When love begins to sicken and decay
It useth an enforced ceremony.
There are no tricks in plain and simple faith;
25   But hollow men, like horses hot at hand,
Make gallant show and promise of their mettle;
But when they should endure the bloody spur,
They fall their crests and like deceitful jades⁹

                         ⁹worthless horses

Sink in the trial. Comes his army on?
30 LUCILIUS: They mean his night in Sardis to be quarter'd;
The greater part, the horse in general,
Are come with Cassius.   *Low march within.*
BRUTUS: Hark, he is arrived.
March gently on to meet him.

Enter Cassius and his powers.

CASSIUS: Stand, ho!
35 BRUTUS: Stand, ho! Speak the word along.
FIRST SOLDIER: Stand!
SECOND SOLDIER: Stand!
THIRD SOLDIER: Stand!
CASSIUS: Most noble brother, you have done me wrong.

40 BRUTUS: Judge me, you gods! Wrong I mine enemies?
      And, if not so, how should I wrong a brother?
    CASSIUS: Brutus, this sober form of yours hides wrongs,
      And when you do them—
    BRUTUS: Cassius, be content,
45   Speak your griefs softly, I do know you well.
      Before the eyes of both our armies here,
      Which should perceive nothing but love from us,
      Let us not wrangle.[10] Bid them move away;
      Then in my tent, Cassius, enlarge[11] your griefs,
50   And I will give you audience.
    CASSIUS: Pindarus,
      Bid our commanders lead their charges off
      A little from this ground.
    BRUTUS: Lucilius, do you the like, and let no man
55   Come to our tent till we have done our conference.
      Let Lucius and Titinius guard our door.

                        Exeunt [all but] Brutus and Cassius

[10] *argue*
[11] *explain*

[SCENE III
Brutus' tent.]

    CASSIUS: That you have wrong'd me doth appear in this:
      You have condemn'd and noted Lucius Pella
      For taking bribes here of the Sardians,
      Wherein my letters, praying on his side,
5   Because I knew the man, were slighted off.
    BRUTUS: You wrong'd yourself to write in such a case.
    CASSIUS: In such a time as this it is not meet
      That every nice offense[12] should bear his comment.[13]
    BRUTUS: Let me tell you, Cassius, you yourself
10   Are much condemn'd to have an itching palm,
      To sell and mart your offices for gold
      To undeservers.
    CASSIUS: I an itching palm?
      You know that you are Brutus that speaks this,
15   Or, by the gods, this speech were else your last.

[12] *tiny mistake*
[13] *be singled out*

BRUTUS: The name of Cassius honors this corruption,[14]
   And chastisement doth therefore hide his head.[15]

CASSIUS: Chastisement?

BRUTUS: Remember March, the ides of March remember.
20   Did not great Julius bleed for justice' sake?
   What villain touch'd his body, that did stab,
   And not for justice? What, shall one of us,
   That struck the foremost man of all this world
   But for supporting robbers,[16] shall we now
25   Contaminate our fingers with base bribes
   And sell the mighty space of our large honors
   For so much trash as may be grasped thus?
   I had rather be a dog, and bay the moon,
   Than such a Roman.

30 CASSIUS: Brutus, bait not me,
   I'll not endure it. You forget yourself
   To hedge me in. I am a soldier, I,
   Older in practice, abler than yourself
   To make conditions.

35 BRUTUS: Go to, you are not, Cassius.

CASSIUS: I am.

BRUTUS: I say you are not.

CASSIUS: Urge me no more, I shall forget myself;
   Have mind upon your health, tempt me no farther.

40 BRUTUS: Away, slight man!

CASSIUS: Is't possible?

BRUTUS: Hear me, for I will speak.
   Must I give way and room to your rash choler?[17]
   Shall I be frighted when a madman stares?

45 CASSIUS: O gods, ye gods! Must I endure all this?

BRUTUS: All this? Ay, more. Fret till your proud heart break.
   Go show your slaves how choleric you are,
   And make your bondmen tremble. Must I bouge?
   Must I observe you? Must I stand and crouch
50   Under your testy humor? By the gods,
   You shall digest the venom of your spleen,[18]
   Though it do split you, for, from this day forth,
   I'll use you for my mirth, yea, for my laughter,
   When you are waspish.

55 CASSIUS: Is it come to this?

[14]this crime seems just because of your honorable name

[15]you therefore go unpunished

[16]except that he supported people who wanted to deprive the Romans of freedom

[17]quick anger

[18][the spleen was associated with anger]

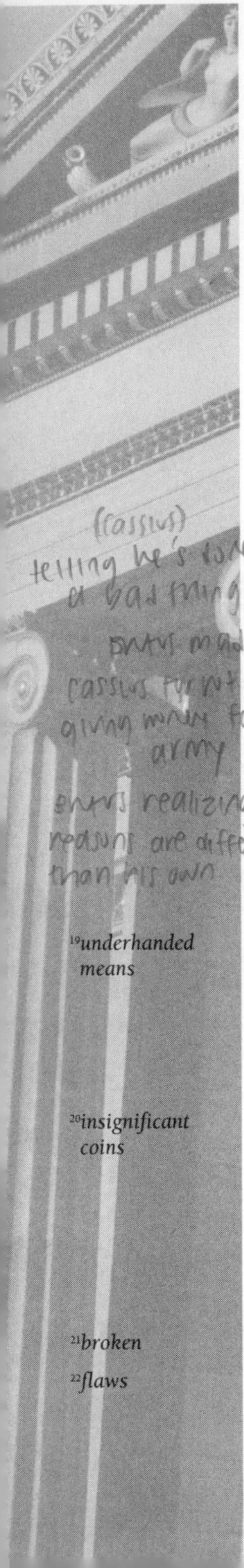

BRUTUS: You say you are a better soldier:
    Let it appear so, make your vaunting true,
    And it shall please me well. For mine own part,
    I shall be glad to learn of noble men.

60 CASSIUS: You wrong me every way, you wrong me, Brutus.
    I said, an elder soldier, not a better.
    Did I say "better"?
BRUTUS: If you did, I care not.
CASSIUS: When Caesar lived, he durst not thus have moved me.
65 BRUTUS: Peace, peace! You durst not so have tempted him.
CASSIUS: I durst not?
BRUTUS: No.
CASSIUS: What, durst not tempt him?
BRUTUS: For your life you durst not.
70 CASSIUS: Do not presume too much upon my love;
    I may do that I shall be sorry for.
BRUTUS: You have done that you should be sorry for.
    There is no terror, Cassius, in your threats,
    For I am arm'd so strong in honesty,
75   That they pass by me as the idle wind
    Which I respect not. I did send to you
    For certain sums of gold, which you denied me,
    For I can raise no money by vile means.
    By heaven, I had rather coin my heart
80   And drop my blood for drachmas than to wring
    From the hard hands of peasants their vile trash
    By any indirection.[19] I did send
    To you for gold to pay my legions,
    Which you denied me. Was that done like Cassius?
85   Should I have answer'd Caius Cassius so?
    When Marcus Brutus grows so covetous
    To lock such rascal counters[20] from his friends,
    Be ready, gods, with all your thunderbolts,
    Dash him to pieces!
90 CASSIUS: I denied you not.
BRUTUS: You did.
CASSIUS: I did not. He was but a fool
    That brought my answer back. Brutus hath rived[21] my heart.
    A friend should bear his friend's infirmities,[22]
95   But Brutus makes mine greater than they are.

[19]underhanded means

[20]insignificant coins

[21]broken

[22]flaws

Handwritten annotations:
- (Cassius) telling he's done a bad thing
- Brutus mad at Cassius for not giving money for army
- Brutus realizing Cassius reasons are different than his own
- not being manipulated by Cassius anymore
- not really meant to work together
- greedy

BRUTUS: I do not, till you practise them on me.

CASSIUS: You love me not.

BRUTUS:　　　　　　　　　I do not like your faults.

CASSIUS: A friendly eye could never see such faults.

100　BRUTUS: A flatterer's would not, though they do appear

As huge as high Olympus.

CASSIUS: Come, Antony, and young Octavius, come,

Revenge yourselves alone on Cassius,

For Cassius is aweary of the world:

105　Hated by one he loves; braved[23] by his brother;

Check'd like a bondman; all his faults observed,

Set in a notebook, learn'd and conn'd[24] by rote,[25] *saying 'go*

To cast into my teeth. O, I could weep *ahead kill me'*

My spirit from mine eyes! There is my dagger,

110　And here my naked breast; within, a heart

Dearer than Pluto's[26] mine, richer than gold.

If that thou best a Roman, take it forth;

I, that denied thee gold, will give my heart.

Strike, as thou didst at Caesar, for I know,

115　When thou didst hate him worst, thou lovedst him better

Than ever thou lovedst Cassius.

BRUTUS:　　　　　　　　　Sheathe your dagger.

Be angry when you will, it shall have scope;[27]

Do what you will, dishonor shall be humor.[28]

120　O Cassius, you are yoked with a lamb,

That carries anger as the flint bears fire,

Who, much enforced, shows a hasty spark

And straight is cold again.

CASSIUS:　　　　　　　　　Hath Cassius lived

125　To be but mirth and laughter to his Brutus,

When grief and blood ill-temper'd vexeth him?

BRUTUS: When I spoke that, I was ill-temper'd too.

CASSIUS: Do you confess so much? Give me your hand. *- be friends*

BRUTUS: And my heart too.

130　CASSIUS:　　　　O Brutus!

BRUTUS:　　　　　What's the matter? *Brutus &*

CASSIUS: Have not you love enough to bear with me, *Cassius are*

When that rash humor[29] which my mother gave me *friends again*

Makes me forgetful?

135　BRUTUS:　　　Yes, Cassius, and from henceforth,

[23]*contradicted*

[24]*learned*

[25]*memorized*

[26]*Plutus, god of wealth.*

[27]*be allowed*

[28]*insults will be attributed to your bad mood*

[29]*quick temper*

When you are overearnest with your Brutus,
He'll think your mother chides, and leave you so.

Enter a Poet.

POET: Let me go in to see the generals.
There is some grudge between 'em, 'tis not meet
140   They be alone.
LUCILIUS: You shall not come to them.
POET: Nothing but death shall stay me.
CASSIUS: How now, what's the matter?
POET: For shame, you generals! What do you mean?
145   Love, and be friends, as two such men should be;
For I have seen more years, I'm sure, than ye.
CASSIUS: Ha, ha! How vilely doth this cynic rhyme!
BRUTUS: Get you hence, sirrah; saucy fellow, hence!
CASSIUS: Bear with him, Brutus; 'tis his fashion.
150 BRUTUS: I'll know his humor when he knows his time.
What should the wars do with these jigging fools?
Companion, hence!
CASSIUS: Away, away, be gone!   *Exit Poet.*
BRUTUS: *[Calling out]* Lucilius and Titinius, bid the commanders
155   Prepare to lodge their companies tonight.
CASSIUS: And come yourselves and bring Messala with you
Immediately to us.
BRUTUS: *[Calling out]* Lucius, a bowl of wine!
CASSIUS: I did not think you could have been so angry.
160 BRUTUS: O Cassius, I am sick of many griefs.
CASSIUS: Of your philosophy you make no use,
If you give place to accidental[30] evils.
BRUTUS: No man bears sorrow better. Portia is dead.
CASSIUS: Ha? Portia?
165 BRUTUS: She is dead.
CASSIUS: How 'scaped killing when I cross'd you so?
O insupportable and touching loss!
Upon what sickness?
BRUTUS: Impatient of my absence,
170   And grief that young Octavius with Mark Antony
Have made themselves so strong:[31] for with her death

[30] *[Brutus is supposed to be a follower of Stoicism, a Greek philosophy that emphasizes evenness of mind in the face of events outside one's control]*

[31] *[Portia was unable to bear both Brutus' absence and the news of Octavius and Antony's victory]*

Portia committed suicide

That tidings came:[32] with this she fell distract,
And, her attendants absent, swallow'd fire.

CASSIUS: And died so?

175 BRUTUS: Even so.

CASSIUS: O ye immortal gods!

Enter [Lucius] with wine, and tapers.

BRUTUS: Speak no more of her. Give me a bowl of wine.
In this I bury all unkindness, Cassius.   *Drinks.*

CASSIUS: My heart is thirsty for that noble pledge.

180   Fill, Lucius, till the wine o'erswell the cup;
I cannot drink too much of Brutus' love.   *[Exit Lucius.]*

Enter Titinius and Messala.

BRUTUS: Come in, Titinius!
               Welcome, good Messala.
Now sit we close about this taper here,

185   And call in question our necessities.

CASSIUS: Portia, art thou gone?

BRUTUS: No more, I pray you.
Messala, I have here received letters
That young Octavius and Mark Antony

190   Come down upon us with a mighty power,
Bending their expedition toward Philippi.

MESSALA: Myself have letters of the selfsame tenure.[33]

BRUTUS: With what addition?

MESSALA: That by proscription and bills of outlawry

195   Octavius, Antony, and Lepidus
Have put to death an hundred senators.

BRUTUS: Therein our letters do not well agree;
Mine speak of seventy senators that died
By their proscriptions, Cicero being one.

200 CASSIUS: Cicero one!

MESSALA: Cicero is dead,
And by that order of proscription.
Had you your letters from your wife, my lord?[34]

BRUTUS: No, Messala.

---

[32] [the news of the victory came along with news of her death, so Brutus deduces that the announcement contributed to her suicide]

[33] meaning

[34] lines 204-219 may be included by mistake, since they repeat the information given in 163

205   Messala: Nor nothing in your letters writ of her?

     Brutus: Nothing, Messala.

     Messala: That, methinks, is strange.

     Brutus: Why ask you? Hear you ought of her in yours?

     Messala: No, my lord.

210   Brutus: Now, as you are a Roman, tell me true.

     Messala: Then like a Roman bear the truth I tell:

       For certain she is dead, and by strange manner.

     Brutus: Why, farewell, Portia. We must die, Messala.

       With meditating that she must die once

215   I have the patience to endure it now.

     Messala: Even so great men great losses should endure.

     Cassius: I have as much of this in art as you,

       But yet my nature could not bear it so.

     Brutus: Well, to our work alive. What do you think

220   Of marching to Philippi presently?

     Cassius: I do not think it good.

     Brutus: Your reason?

     Cassius: This it is:

       'Tis better that the enemy seek us;

225   So shall he waste his means, weary his soldiers,

       Doing himself offense, whilst we lying still

       Are full of rest, defense, and nimbleness.

     Brutus: Good reasons must of force[35] give place to better.

       The people 'twixt Philippi and this ground

230   Do stand but in a forced affection,[36]

       For they have grudged us contribution.[37]

       The enemy, marching along by them,

       By them shall make a fuller number up,

       Come on refresh'd, new-added, and encouraged;

235   From which advantage shall we cut him off

       If at Philippi we do face him there,

       These people at our back.

     Cassius: Hear me, good brother.

     Brutus: Under your pardon. You must note beside

240   That we have tried the utmost of our friends,

       Our legions[38] are brim-full, our cause is ripe:

       The enemy increaseth every day;

       We, at the height, are ready to decline.

       There is a tide in the affairs of men

[35]necessarily

[36]support of us

[37]gave us help only reluctantly

[38]troops

245 Which taken at the flood leads on to fortune;
Omitted, all the voyage of their life
Is bound in shallows and in miseries.
On such a full sea are we now afloat,
And we must take the current when it serves,
250 Or lose our ventures.
CASSIUS: Then, with your will, go on;
We'll along ourselves and meet them at Philippi.
BRUTUS: The deep of night is crept upon our talk,
And nature must obey necessity,
255 Which we will niggard[39] with a little rest.
There is no more to say?
CASSIUS: No more. Good night.
Early tomorrow will we rise and hence.
BRUTUS: Lucius! *Enter Lucius.* My gown.   *[Exit Lucius.]*
260 Farewell, good Messala;
Good night, Titinius; noble, noble Cassius,
Good night and good repose.
CASSIUS: O my dear brother!
This was an ill beginning of the night.
265 Never come such division 'tween our souls!
Let it not, Brutus.

Enter Lucius, with the gown.

BRUTUS: Every thing is well.
CASSIUS: Good night, my lord.
BRUTUS: Good night, good brother.
270 TITINIUS AND MESSALA: Good night, Lord Brutus.
BRUTUS: Farewell, everyone.   *Exeunt [all but Brutus.]*
Give me the gown. Where is thy instrument?
LUCIUS: Here in the tent.
BRUTUS: What, thou speak'st drowsily?
275 Poor knave, I blame thee not, thou art o'erwatch'd.[40]
Call Claudius and some other of my men,
I'll have them sleep on cushions in my tent.
LUCIUS: Varro and Claudio!

Enter Varro and Claudio.

[39]*give only a little to*

[40]*tired from standing guard too long*

VARRO: Calls my lord?

280 BRUTUS: I pray you, sirs, lie in my tent and sleep;
    It may be I shall raise you by and by
    On business to my brother Cassius.

VARRO: So please you, we will stand and watch your pleasure.

BRUTUS: I will not have it so. Lie down, good sirs.
285   It may be I shall otherwise bethink me.

                    [Varro and Claudio lie down.]

    Look, Lucius, here's the book I sought for so;
    I put it in the pocket of my gown.

LUCIUS: I was sure your lordship did not give it me.

BRUTUS: Bear with me, good boy, I am much forgetful.
290   Canst thou hold up thy heavy eyes a while,
    And touch thy instrument a strain[41] or two?

LUCIUS: Ay, my lord, an't please you.

BRUTUS: It does, my boy.
    I trouble thee too much, but thou art willing.

295 LUCIUS: It is my duty, sir.

BRUTUS: I should not urge thy duty past thy might;
    I know young bloods look for a time of rest.

LUCIUS: I have slept, my lord, already.

BRUTUS: It was well done, and thou shalt sleep again;
300   I will not hold thee long. If I do live,
    I will be good to thee.   *Music, and a song.*
    This is a sleepy tune. O murderous slumber,
    Layest thou thy leaden mace upon my boy

                    [Lucius falls asleep]

    That plays thee music? Gentle knave, good night.
305   I will not do thee so much wrong to wake thee.
    If thou dost nod, thou break'st thy instrument;
    I'll take it from thee; and, good boy, good night.
    Let me see, let me see; is not the leaf turn'd down
    Where I left reading? Here it is, I think.

Enter the Ghost of Caesar.

310   How ill this taper burns! Ha, who comes here?
    I think it is the weakness of mine eyes
    That shapes this monstrous apparition.
    It comes upon me. Art thou any thing?
    Art thou some god, some angel, or some devil

[41]*song*

315   That makest my blood cold, and my hair to stare?
       Speak to me what thou art.
       GHOST: Thy evil spirit, Brutus.
       BRUTUS: Why comest thou?
       GHOST: To tell thee thou shalt see me at Philippi.
320   BRUTUS: Well, then I shall see thee again?
       GHOST: Ay, at Philippi.
       BRUTUS: Why, I will see thee at Philippi then.   *[Exit Ghost.]*
       Now I have taken heart thou vanishest.
       Ill spirit, I would hold more talk with thee.
325   Boy, Lucius! Varro! Claudius! Sirs, awake!
       Claudius!
       LUCIUS: The strings, my lord, are false.
       BRUTUS: He thinks he still is at his instrument.
       Lucius, awake!
330   LUCIUS: My lord?
       BRUTUS: Didst thou dream, Lucius, that thou so criedst out?
       LUCIUS: My lord, I do not know that I did cry.
       BRUTUS: Yes, that thou didst. Didst thou see any thing?
       LUCIUS: Nothing, my lord.
335   BRUTUS: Sleep again, Lucius. Sirrah Claudius!
       [To Varro.] Fellow thou, awake!
       VARRO: My lord?
       CLAUDIUS: My lord?
       BRUTUS: Why did you so cry out, sirs, in your sleep?
340   VARRO AND CLAUDIUS: Did we, my lord?
       BRUTUS: Ay, saw you any thing?
       VARRO: No, my lord, I saw nothing.
       CLAUDIUS: Nor I, my lord.
       BRUTUS: Go and commend me to my brother Cassius;
345   Bid him set on his powers[42] betimes before,
       And we will follow.
       VARRO AND CLAUDIUS: It shall be done, my lord.

                                              Exeunt.

[42]*forces*

ACT V
JULIUS CAESAR

ACT V

[SCENE I
The plains of Philippi.]

Enter Octavius, Antony, and their Army.

OCTAVIUS: Now, Antony, our hopes are answered.
   You said the enemy would not come down,
   But keep the hills and upper regions.
   It proves not so. Their battles are at hand;
5   They mean to warn us at Philippi here,
   Answering[1] before we do demand of[2] them.
ANTONY: Tut, I am in their bosoms,[3] and I know
   Wherefore they do it. They could be content
   To visit other places,[4] and come down
10   With fearful bravery, thinking by this face
   To fasten in our thoughts that they have courage;
   But 'tis not so.

Enter a Messenger.

MESSALA: Prepare you, generals.
   The enemy comes on in gallant show;
15   Their bloody sign of battle is hung out,
   And something to be done immediately.
ANTONY: Octavius, lead your battle softly on,
   Upon the left hand of the even field.
OCTAVIUS: Upon the right hand I, keep thou the left.
20 ANTONY: Why do you cross me in this exigent?[5]
OCTAVIUS: I do not cross you, but I will do so.   *March.*

Drum. Enter Brutus, Cassius, and their Army [Lucilius, Titinius, Messala, and others.]

[1] *responding to us*
[2] *attack*
[3] *I know their hearts*
[4] *want to be somewhere else*
[5] *urgent matter*

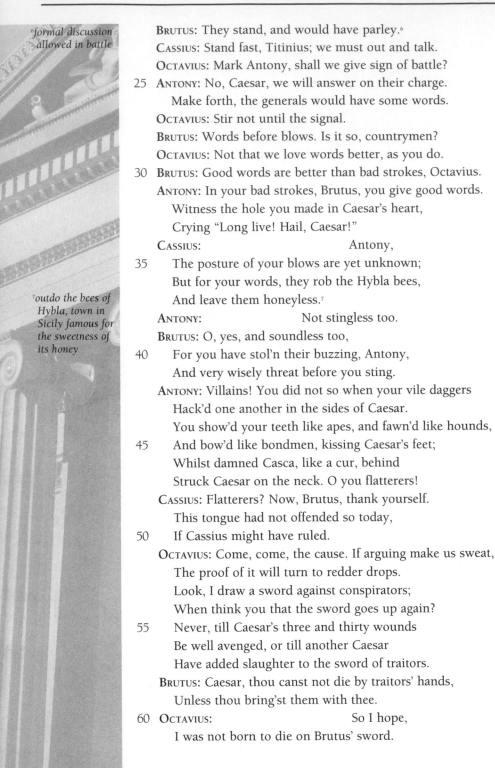

⁶formal discussion allowed in battle

⁷outdo the bees of Hybla, town in Sicily famous for the sweetness of its honey

BRUTUS: They stand, and would have parley.⁶

CASSIUS: Stand fast, Titinius; we must out and talk.

OCTAVIUS: Mark Antony, shall we give sign of battle?

25 ANTONY: No, Caesar, we will answer on their charge.

     Make forth, the generals would have some words.

OCTAVIUS: Stir not until the signal.

BRUTUS: Words before blows. Is it so, countrymen?

OCTAVIUS: Not that we love words better, as you do.

30 BRUTUS: Good words are better than bad strokes, Octavius.

ANTONY: In your bad strokes, Brutus, you give good words.

     Witness the hole you made in Caesar's heart,

     Crying "Long live! Hail, Caesar!"

CASSIUS: Antony,

35   The posture of your blows are yet unknown;

     But for your words, they rob the Hybla bees,

     And leave them honeyless.⁷

ANTONY: Not stingless too.

BRUTUS: O, yes, and soundless too,

40   For you have stol'n their buzzing, Antony,

     And very wisely threat before you sting.

ANTONY: Villains! You did not so when your vile daggers

     Hack'd one another in the sides of Caesar.

     You show'd your teeth like apes, and fawn'd like hounds,

45   And bow'd like bondmen, kissing Caesar's feet;

     Whilst damned Casca, like a cur, behind

     Struck Caesar on the neck. O you flatterers!

CASSIUS: Flatterers? Now, Brutus, thank yourself.

     This tongue had not offended so today,

50   If Cassius might have ruled.

OCTAVIUS: Come, come, the cause. If arguing make us sweat,

     The proof of it will turn to redder drops.

     Look, I draw a sword against conspirators;

     When think you that the sword goes up again?

55   Never, till Caesar's three and thirty wounds

     Be well avenged, or till another Caesar

     Have added slaughter to the sword of traitors.

  BRUTUS: Caesar, thou canst not die by traitors' hands,

     Unless thou bring'st them with thee.

60 OCTAVIUS: So I hope,

     I was not born to die on Brutus' sword.

BRUTUS: O, if thou wert the noblest of thy strain,
    Young man, thou couldst not die more honorable.
CASSIUS: A peevish school boy, worthless of such honor,
65   Join'd with a masker and a reveller![8]
ANTONY: Old Cassius still!
OCTAVIUS: Come, Antony, away!
    Defiance, traitors, hurl we in your teeth.
    If you dare fight today, come to the field;
70   If not, when you have stomachs.[9]
                  Exeunt Octavius, Antony, and Army.
CASSIUS: Why, now, blow and, swell billow, and swim bark!
    The storm is up, and all is on the hazard.[10]
BRUTUS: Ho, Lucilius! Hark, a word with you.
LUCILIUS: My lord?
               Lucilius and Messala stand forth.
75 CASSIUS: Messala!
MESSALA: What says my general?
CASSIUS: Messala,
    This is my birthday, as this very day
    Was Cassius born. Give me thy hand, Messala.
80   Be thou my witness that, against my will,
    As Pompey was, am I compell'd to set
    Upon one battle all our liberties.
    You know that I held Epicurus[11] strong,
    And his opinion. Now I change my mind,
85   And partly credit things that do presage.[12]
    Coming from Sardis, on our former[13] ensign[14]
    Two mighty eagles fell, and there they perch'd,
    Gorging and feeding from our soldiers' hands,
    Who to Philippi here consorted[15] us.
90   This morning are they fled away and gone,
    And in their steads do ravens, crows, and kites
    Fly o'er our heads and downward look on us,
    As we were sickly prey. Their shadows seem
    A canopy most fatal, under which
95   Our army lies, ready to give up the ghost.
MESSALA: Believe not so.
CASSIUS: I but believe it partly,
    For I am fresh of spirit and resolved
    To meet all perils very constantly.[16]

[8] *loose party-lover*

[9] *are brave enough*

[10] *at risk*

[11] *a Greek philosopher who scorned belief in omens and superstitions*

[12] *tell the future*

[13] *leading*

[14] *military banner*

[15] *came with*

[16] *with an even mind*

100   BRUTUS: Even so, Lucilius.

CASSIUS: Now, most noble Brutus,
     The gods today stand friendly, that we may,
     Lovers in peace, lead on our days to age!
     But, since the affairs of men rest still incertain,
105   Let's reason with the worst that may befall.
     If we do lose this battle, then is this
     The very last time we shall speak together.
     What are you then determined to do?

BRUTUS: Even by the rule of that philosophy
110   By which I did blame Cato for the death
     Which he did give himself: I know not how,
     But I do find it cowardly and vile,
     For fear of what might fall, so to prevent
     The time of life: arming myself with patience
115   To stay the providence of some high powers
     That govern us below.

CASSIUS: Then, if we lose this battle,
     You are contented to be led in triumph[17]
     Thorough the streets of Rome?

120   BRUTUS: No, Cassius, no. Think not, thou noble Roman,
     That ever Brutus will go bound to Rome;
     He bears too great a mind. But this same day
     Must end that work the ides of March begun.
     And whether we shall meet again I know not.
125   Therefore our everlasting farewell take.
     For ever, and for ever, farewell, Cassius!
     If we do meet again, why, we shall smile;
     If not, why then this parting was well made.

CASSIUS: For ever and for ever farewell, Brutus!
130   If we do meet again, we'll smile indeed;
     If not, 'tis true this parting was well made.

BRUTUS: Why then, lead on. O, that a man might know
     The end of this day's business ere it come!
     But it sufficeth that the day will end,
135   And then the end is known. Come, ho! Away!

Exeunt.

[17] *led as a captive in a procession*

[SCENE II
The field of battle.]

[handwritten: Gives Messala a letter to give to Cassius to attack b/c he sees weakness in Octavius' army.]

Alarum. Enter Brutus and Messala.

BRUTUS: Ride, ride, Messala, ride, and give these bills[18]
    Unto the legions on the other side.   *Loud alarum.*
    Let them set on at once, for I perceive
    But cold demeanor[19] in Octavius' wing,
5   And sudden push gives them the overthrow.[20]
    Ride, ride, Messala. Let them all come down.

                        Exeunt.

[18]*written commands*

[19]*sluggish spirit*

[20]*a quick attack will defeat them*

[SCENE III
Another part of the field.]

[handwritten: Cassius sends Pindarus to see what is going on. He finds Titinius is captured and kills himself and Titinius kills himself too after seeing Cassius.]

Alarums. Enter Cassius and Titinius.

CASSIUS: O, look, Titinius, look, the villains fly!
    Myself have to mine own turn'd enemy.
    This ensign here of mine was turning back;
    I slew the coward, and did take it from him.
5 TITINIUS: O Cassius, Brutus gave the word too early,
    Who, having some advantage on Octavius,
    Took it too eagerly. His soldiers fell to spoil,
    Whilst we by Antony are all enclosed.

Enter Pindarus.

PINDARUS: Fly further off, my lord, fly further off;
10   Mark Antony is in your tents, my lord;
    Fly, therefore, noble Cassius, fly far off.
CASSIUS: This hill is far enough. Look, look, Titinius:
    Are those my tents where I perceive the fire?
TITINIUS: They are, my lord.
15 CASSIUS: Titinius, if thou lovest me,
    Mount thou my horse and hide thy spurs in him,
    Till he have brought thee up to yonder troops
    And here again, that I may rest assured

       Whether yond troops are friend or enemy.

20 TITINIUS: I will be here again, even with a thought.   *Exit.*

    CASSIUS: Go, Pindarus, get higher on that hill;

       My sight was ever thick; regard Titinius,

       And tell me what thou notest about the field.

    [Pindarus ascends.]

       This day I breathed first: time is come round,

25   And where I did begin, there shall I end;

       My life is run his compass. Sirrah, what news?

    PINDARUS: *Above.* O my lord!

    CASSIUS: What news?

    PINDARUS: *[Above.]* Titinius is enclosed round about

30   With horsemen, that make to him on the spur;[21]

       Yet he spurs on. Now they are almost on him.

       Now, Titinius! Now some light. O, he lights too.

       He's ta'en *Shout.* And, hark! They shout for joy.

    CASSIUS: Come down; behold no more.

35   O, coward that I am, to live so long,

       To see my best friend ta'en before my face!

    Enter Pindarus [from above.]

       Come hither, sirrah.

       In Parthia did I take thee prisoner,

       And then I swore thee, saving of thy life,

40   That whatsoever I did bid thee do,

       Thou shouldst attempt it. Come now, keep thine oath;

       Now be a freeman, and with this good sword,

       That ran through Caesar's bowels, search this bosom.

       Stand not to answer: here, take thou the hilts;

45   And when my face is cover'd, as 'tis now,

       Guide thou the sword.   *[Pindarus stabs him.]*

              Caesar, thou art revenged,

       Even with the sword that kill'd thee.   *[Dies.]*

    PINDARUS: So, I am free, yet would not so have been,

50   Durst I have done my will. O Cassius!

       Far from this country Pindarus shall run,

       Where never Roman shall take note of him.   *[Exit.]*

    [Re-]Enter Titinius and Messala. [earing the laurels.]

    MESSALA: It is but change, Titinius, for Octavius

       Is overthrown by noble Brutus' power,

[21] *gallop towards him*

55   As Cassius' legions are by Antony.
        TITINIUS: These tidings would well comfort Cassius.
        MESSALA: Where did you leave him?
        TITINIUS: All disconsolate,
            With Pindarus his bondman, on this hill.
60   MESSALA: Is not that he that lies upon the ground?
        TITINIUS: He lies not like the living. O my heart!
        MESSALA: Is not that he?
        TITINIUS: No, this was he, Messala,
            But Cassius is no more. O setting sun,
65   As in thy red rays thou dost sink to night,
            So in his red blood Cassius' day is set,
            The sun of Rome is set! Our day is gone;
            Clouds, dews, and dangers come; our deeds are done!
            Mistrust of my success hath done this deed.
70   MESSALA: Mistrust of good success hath done this deed.
            O hateful error, melancholy's child,
            Why dost thou show to the apt[22] thoughts of men
            The things that are not? O error, soon conceived,
            Thou never comest unto a happy birth,
75   But kill'st the mother that engender'd[23] thee!
        TITINIUS: What, Pindarus! Where art thou, Pindarus?
        MESSALA: Seek him, Titinius, whilst I go to meet
            The noble Brutus, thrusting this report
            Into his ears. I may say "thrusting" it,
80   For piercing steel and darts envenomed
            Shall be as welcome to the ears of Brutus
            As tidings of this sight.
        TITINIUS: Hie you, Messala,
            And I will seek for Pindarus the while.   *[Exit Messala.]*
85   Why didst thou send me forth, brave Cassius?
            Did I not meet thy friends? And did not they
            Put on my brows this wreath of victory,
            And bid me give it thee? Didst thou not hear their shouts?
            Alas, thou hast misconstrued every thing!
90   But, hold thee, take this garland on thy brow;
            Thy Brutus bid me give it thee, and I
            Will do his bidding. Brutus, come apace,
            And see how I regarded Caius Cassius.
            By your leave, gods, this is a Roman's part.
95   Come, Cassius' sword, and find Titinius' heart.   *Dies.*

[22]*easily changed*

[23]*gave birth to*

[Alarum. Enter Brutus, Messala, young Cato, Strato, Volumnius, and Lucilius [Labeo, and Flavius.]

BRUTUS: Where, where, Messala, doth his body lie?
MESSALA: Lo, yonder, and Titinius mourning it.
BRUTUS: Titinius' face is upward.
CATO: He is slain.
100 BRUTUS: O Julius Caesar, thou art mighty yet!
    Thy spirit walks abroad, and turns our swords
    In our own proper entrails.   *Low alarums.*
CATO: Brave Titinius!
    Look whether he have not crown'd dead Cassius!
105 BRUTUS: Are yet two Romans living such as these?
    The last of all the Romans, fare thee well!
    It is impossible that ever Rome
    Should breed thy fellow. Friends, I owe more tears
    To this dead man than you shall see me pay.
110   I shall find time, Cassius, I shall find time.
    Come therefore, and to Thasos send his body;
    His funerals shall not be in our camp,
    Lest it discomfort us. Lucilius, come,
    And come, young Cato; let us to the field.
115   Labeo and Flavius, set our battles on.
    'Tis three o'clock, and Romans, yet ere night
    We shall try fortune in a second fight.
                                   Exeunt.

[SCENE IV
Another part of the field.]

Cato pretends to be Brutus and gets captured and killed

Alarum. Enter Messala, Cato, Lucilius, and Flavius.]

BRUTUS: Yet, countrymen, O, yet hold up your heads!   *[Exit.]*
CATO: What bastard doth not? Who will go with me?
    I will proclaim my name about the field.
    I am the son of Marcus Cato, ho!
5   A foe to tyrants, and my country's friend.
    I am the son of Marcus Cato, ho!

Enter Soldiers and fight.

Lucilius: And I am Brutus, Marcus Brutus, I;[24]
    Brutus, my country's friend; know me for Brutus!
                              [Young Cato is slain.]
    O young and noble Cato, art thou down?
10   Why, now thou diest as bravely as Titinius,
    And mayst be honor'd, being Cato's son.
First Soldier: Yield, or thou diest.
Lucilius: Only I yield to die.   *[Offers money.]*
    There is so much that thou wilt kill me straight:
15   Kill Brutus, and be honor'd in his death.
First Soldier: We must not. A noble prisoner!

Enter Antony.

Second Soldier: Room, ho! Tell Antony, Brutus is ta'en.
First Soldier: I'll tell the news. Here comes the general.
    Brutus is ta'en, Brutus is ta'en, my lord.
20 Antony: Where is he?
Lucilius: Safe, Antony, Brutus is safe enough.
    I dare assure thee that no enemy
    Shall ever take alive the noble Brutus;
    The gods defend him from so great a shame!
25   When you do find him, or alive or dead,
    He will be found like Brutus, like himself.
Antony: This is not Brutus, friend, but, I assure you,
    A prize no less in worth. Keep this man safe,
    Give him all kindness; I had rather have
30   Such men my friends than enemies. Go on,
    And see whether Brutus be alive or dead,
    And bring us word unto Octavius' tent
    How every thing is chanced.   *Exeunt.*

[24] *[Lucilius imper-sonates Brutus]*

*Brutus kills himself
after Cassius & Titinus
kill themselve. Antony
praises Brutus
for his honor.*

[SCENE V
Another part of the field.]

Enter Brutus, Dardanius, Clitus, Strato, and Volumnius.

BRUTUS: Come, poor remains of friends, rest on this rock.

CLITUS: Statilius show'd the torch-light, but, my lord,
     He came not back. He is or ta'en or slain.

BRUTUS: Sit thee down, Clitus. Slaying is the word:

5   It is a deed in fashion.[25] Hark thee, Clitus.

[25] popular activity

CLITUS: What, I, my lord? No, not for all the world.

BRUTUS: Peace then, no words.

CLITUS: I'll rather kill myself.

BRUTUS: Hark thee, Dardanius.

10 DARDANIUS: Shall I do such a deed?

CLITUS: O Dardanius!

DARDANIUS: O Clitus!

CLITUS: What ill request did Brutus make to thee?

DARDANIUS: To kill him, Clitus. Look, he meditates.

15 CLITUS: Now is that noble vessel full of grief,
     That it runs over even at his eyes.

BRUTUS: Come hither, good Volumnius, list a word.

VOLUMNIUS: What says my lord?

BRUTUS: Why, this, Volumnius:

20   The ghost of Caesar hath appear'd to me
     Two several times by night; at Sardis once,
     And this last night here in Philippi fields.
     I know my hour is come.

VOLUMNIUS: Not so, my lord.

25 BRUTUS: Nay, I am sure it is, Volumnius.
     Thou seest the world, Volumnius, how it goes;
     Our enemies have beat us to the pit;   *Low alarums.*
     It is more worthy to leap in ourselves
     Than tarry till they push us. Good Volumnius,

30   Thou know'st that we two went to school together;
     Even for that our love of old, I prithee,
     Hold thou my sword-hilts, whilst I run on it.

VOLUMNIUS: That's not an office for a friend, my lord.

                                Alarum still.

CLITUS: Fly, fly, my lord, there is no tarrying here.

35　BRUTUS: Farewell to you, and you, and you, Volumnius.
　　　　Strato, thou hast been all this while asleep;
　　　　Farewell to thee too, Strato. Countrymen,
　　　　My heart doth joy that yet in all my life
　　　　I found no man but he was true to me.
40　　　I shall have glory by this losing day,
　　　　More than Octavius and Mark Antony
　　　　By this vile conquest shall attain unto.
　　　　So, fare you well at once, for Brutus' tongue
　　　　Hath almost ended his life's history.
45　　　Night hangs upon mine eyes, my bones would rest
　　　　That have but labor'd to attain this hour.
　　　　　　　　　　　　　Alarum. Cry within, "Fly, fly, fly!"
　　CLITUS:　Fly, my lord, fly.
　　BRUTUS:　　　　　　　Hence! I will follow.
　　　　　　　[Exeunt Clitus, Dardanius, and
　　　Volumnius.]
50　　　I prithee, Strato, stay thou by thy lord.
　　　　Thou art a fellow of a good respect;
　　　　Thy life hath had some[26] smatch[27] of honor in it.
　　　　Hold then my sword, and turn away thy face,
　　　　While I do run upon it. Wilt thou, Strato?
55　STRATO:　Give me your hand first. Fare you well, my lord.
　　BRUTUS: Farewell, good Strato.　　　　　*[Runs on his sword.]*
　　　　Caesar, now be still;
　　　　I kill'd not thee with half so good a will.　　　*Dies.*

*Alarum. Retreat. Enter Antony, Octavius, Messala, Lucilius, and
the Army.*

　　OCTAVIUS: What man is that?
60　MESSALA:　My master's man. Strato, where is thy master?
　　STRATO:　Free from the bondage you are in, Messala:
　　　　The conquerors can but make a fire of him;
　　　　For Brutus only overcame himself,
　　　　And no man else hath honor by his death.
65　LUCILIUS: So Brutus should be found. I thank thee, Brutus,
　　　　That thou hast proved Lucilius' saying true.
　　OCTAVIUS: All that served Brutus, I will entertain[28] them.
　　　　Fellow, wilt thou bestow[29] thy time with me?
　　STRATO:　Ay, if Messala will prefer[30] me to you.

[26]*at least some*
[27]*small amount*

[28]*employ*
[29]*give*
[30]*recommend*

OCTAVIUS: Do so, good Messala.

70 MESSALA: How died my master, Strato?

STRATO: I held the sword, and he did run on it.

MESSALA: Octavius, then take him to follow thee

    That did the latest service to my master.

ANTONY: This was the noblest Roman of them all.

75   All the conspirators, save only he,

    Did that they did in envy of great Caesar;

    He only, in a general honest thought

    And common good to all, made one of them.

    His life was gentle, and the elements

80   So mix'd in him that Nature might stand up

    And say to all the world, "This was a man!"

OCTAVIUS: According to his virtue let us use him

    With all respect and rites of burial.

    Within my tent his bones tonight shall lie,

85   Most like a soldier, order'd honorably.

    So call the field to rest, and let's away,

    To part[31] the glories of this happy day.

                                      Exeunt.

[31]*share*

THE END

Themes

- how easily manipulated people are _changeable_
- what happens when you question authority
  when to question?
- fight for power — conspirators & Caesar
  Antony & Octavius & Lepidus
- pandora's box - once you question, chaos happens
- mob - chaotic dangerous
- personal vs. public
- Brutus' honor - how if causes biggest
  heights and downfalls

Brutus & Caesar - similar, think public self
invincible, what leads to their demise

VOCABULARY AND GLOSSARY

Act I, scene i
battlements—a castle or fortress walls, with openings for shooting
concave—curved inwardly
knave—rascal
mechanical— a tradesman
oft—often
tributaries—rulers who serve

Act I, scene ii
an—if
aught—anything
become—suit
bestride—straddle
ere—before
fain—gladly
gamesome—enjoying sports or festivities
lief—rather
loath—reluctant
mark—notice
marry—by the Virgin Mary (an oath)
mettle—temperament
rabblement—common people
soothsayer—a prophet
spare—lean
start—raise
tardy—slow, dull

Act I, scene iii
close—hidden
gait—manner of walking
heralds—messengers
hie—go on
hinds—female deer; servants
pleasure—will
saucy—disobedient
save—except
stay'd—waited
tempest—a storm
tokens—omens
wonderful—amazing

Act II, scene i
affability—amiability
affections—emotions
base—lowly
betimes—early
closet—a private chamber
disjoins—separates
faction—a group of people
fret—to streak
hew—cut
rated—berated, criticized
sound—try
toils—nets
withal—besides
withal—nonetheless

Act II, scene ii
ague—fever, sickness
amiss—wrongly
expounded—explained
portents—omens
whelped—given birth
yearns—grieves

Act II, scene iii
contrive—conspire
emulation—envy

Act II, scene iv
doth—does
enterprise—a significant undertaking
ere—before
sooth—in truth
yet—still

Act III, scene i
being prostrate—lying on my face
carrion—something that is disgusting
confounded—bewildered
cur—a dog
enfranchisement—reinstatement of rights
fell—cruel
Sirrah—used to address a person of lower rank
firmament—the sky

fond—foolish
"Havoc"—battle cry that signals a period of unlimited killing
pulpit—a raised platform
vouchsafe—swear

Act III, scene ii
arbors—trees
base—low in status
censure—judge
drachmas—silver Greek coins
enrolled—recorded in documents
meet—fitting

Act IV, scene i
crests—heads
divers—diverse; many
enforced ceremony—forced politeness
jades—worn-out horses
or...or—either...or
pricked—written with a quill pen
proscription—the condition of being outlawed or exiled

Act IV, scene ii
resolved—informed
stand—halt

Act IV, scene iii
bay—to howl
choleric—angry. *Choler*, or yellow bile, is one of the four *humors*—bodily fluids
   that are supposed to determine a person's mood and character, according to
   a theory popular from ancient to Elizabethan times. An excess of yellow bile
   makes a person angry and vengeful; too much black bile results in a *melancholy*,
   or depressed, personality; an abundance of phlegm (mucus) makes for a sluggish and dull nature, called *phlegmatic*; and too much blood results in a *san-*
   guine, or cheerful, type.
durst—dared
jigging—poorly rhyming
nice—minor, insignificant
philosophy—Stoicism, a philosophy founded by the Greek Zeno in 300 B.C.
   Stoicism calls upon its followers to disregard circumstances that are beyond
   their control and temper their emotions. The Romans Seneca and Marcus
   Aurelius were Stoics who stressed moderation and moral correctness. Brutus'
   Stoicism comes out in his indifference to death and in his strict moral guide-
   lines.

rived—split
spleen—the organ that produces bile
vaunting—boasting
waspish—irritable

Act V, scene i
consorted—accompanied
fearful—trying to inspire fear
kites—scavenging birds
on the hazard—at risk
peevish—silly
strain—family
tut—an exclamation showing impatience

Act V, scene ii

——

Act V, scene iii
compass—course
disconsolate—inconsolable
enclosed—surrounded
engender'd—gave birth to
ensign—flag-bearer
spoil—looting
wreath of victory—the symbol of victory was a laurel wreath

Act V, scene v
bestow—spend
entertain—employ
prefer—recommend
tarry—wait

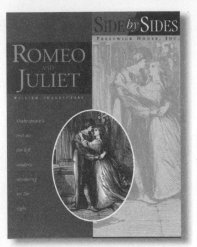